KILLER POLITICS

KILLER POLITICS

How Big Money and Bad Politics
Are Destroying the Great American Middle Class

Ed Schultz

HYPERION

NEW YORK

Library of Congress Cataloging-in-Publication Data

Schultz, Ed.
Killer politics : how big money and bad politics are destroying
the great American middle class / Ed Schultz.
p. cm.
ISBN 978-1-4013-2378-3
1. United States—Politics and government—2009–   2. United States—
Politics and government—2001–2009.   3. United States—
Economic conditions—2009–
4. United States—Economic policy—2009–
5. Fiscal policy—United States.   I. Title.
E907.S38 2010
330.973—dc22
2010000177

Hyperion books are available for special promotions and premiums. For details contact the HarperCollins Special Markets Department in the New York office at 212-207-7528, fax 212-207-7222, or email spsales@harpercollins.com.

Book design by Karen Minster

FIRST EDITION

10 9 8 7 6 5 4 3 2 1

THIS LABEL APPLIES TO TEXT STOCK

We try to produce the most beautiful books possible, and we are also extremely concerned about the impact of our manufacturing process on the forests of the world and the environment as a whole. Accordingly, we've made sure that all of the paper we use has been certified as coming from forests that are managed, to ensure the protection of the people and wildlife dependent upon them.

This book is dedicated to the great middle class,
the heart, soul, and backbone of America
—people I love, support, respect, and admire.

Contents

Acknowledgments

Although the name on the cover of this book is mine, any project of this scope requires a team effort. It started with Will Balliett, who brought this project to Hyperion and placed it in the capable hands of my editor, Barbara Jones. Barbara, a woman of tremendous energy and vision, did a fantastic job of helping us improve the manuscript. I truly appreciated the enthusiasm for this project that I found at Hyperion. These aren't people just looking to churn out another book—these are people who want their work to make a difference. They embraced my message and have worked hard to help me share it.

Special thanks goes to my agent Connie West, the consummate pro, for helping me navigate the literary world, and to my friend and collaborator, Tony Bender, the best writer I know, who did such a great job of helping me organize my thoughts into chapters.

An awful lot of this book originated in conversations with my producer James "Holmie" Holmes and my manager, Vern Thompson, whose research and political instincts are driving factors behind *The Ed Schultz Show*. I don't know what I'd do without Vern and Holmie. They're like loyal black Labs that never get tired of hunting, and if you know anything about me, you know that is high praise.

Vern is the former chairman of the Democratic Party in North Dakota and a former state legislator, and he brings with him remarkable political insight and an unreal work ethic. And Holmie? The man has a black belt in liberalism and has been so loyal he moved his family to New York to make sure somebody had my back. Holmie brings an idealist spirit and a brash energy to the operation.

We might be broadcasting our radio show in every major market in America, and we might have a national television show on MSNBC, but when it comes down to it, this is a mom-and-pop operation. My partner, producer, confidante, wife, and best friend is the amazing Wendy Schultz. She picks me up in the bad times, and she keeps me grounded in the good times. Wendy's influence brings heart to the show. I wouldn't be here without her.

KILLER POLITICS

THERE WAS BLOOD

I WAS BLEEDING.

In 2004, in a make-or-break moment for my career, I launched the Ed Schultz radio show with a bloody nose. Just seconds before I was about to go on the air with my much-publicized effort to challenge the right wing stranglehold on talk radio, my nose began spouting blood like the cannon fodder so many thought I was.

Throughout the radio industry, the conventional wisdom was that liberal talk just couldn't work, and New York's WABC radio general manager Phil Boyce himself, who had launched the career of right wing wonder boy Sean Hannity, said liberal radio didn't have a chance. Rush Limbaugh called me "that little guy from North Dakota."

They were right about one thing. Every liberal talker from Mario Cuomo to Jim Hightower to Alan Dershowitz had failed, but what they didn't get was that it wasn't the message—not in a country equally divided between Republicans and Democrats—it was the messengers. These are all fine men, but they were not radio professionals. I understood that you can write all the great lyrics in the world, but if you want people to listen, you need a great singer. I can't sing, but I damn sure knew I could talk, and that's why I thought I could succeed. I don't think I knew just how hard it would be, though. That bloody nose became a fitting metaphor for what is the fight of our lives—a contest for the soul of America.

The middle class, where the greatness of this nation is rooted, is under siege by an increasingly unethical system, managed by economic vampires who are sucking the lifeblood out of the American family and ripping the heart out of democracy itself. From mortgage scams to credit card predation to health insurance hustles, greed is killing our country.

Despite that bloody nose and an inauspicious start with just two small radio stations—KNDK in Langdon, North Dakota, and KTOX in Needles, California—signed on to my "national show," today, *The Ed Schultz Show* has one hundred affiliates, including XM satellite channel 167. We're in every major market. And since April 2009, *The Ed Show* every weeknight on MSNBC TV has given me another platform to tell it like it is. My on-air presence, along with a rising number of liberal-minded websites and bloggers, has helped balance the national debate and helped Democrats to majorities in Congress and to a historic victory in the White House.

And, of course, we all lived happily ever after.

Wasn't that what was supposed to happen? Well, if anything close to a happy ending had occurred, I'd be on a boat getting sunburned with a beer in one hand and a fishing rod in the other. There would be no need for this book.

Instead, after the inspirational candidacy and election of President Barack Obama, the contest for America's soul has gotten even more malicious than it was when right wingers had a near monopoly on the airwaves. Reasonable Americans find ourselves pitted in an ideological struggle against an extremist right wing movement that really believes greed is good, that money trumps patriotism. Where is their love of country? There can be no compromise with people like that. I wonder if Americans can ever be united again.

You can't just bring those extremists, that corrupt posse, to the White House for a beer summit. You can't take them fishing. Good Lord, anytime you get them near a trout stream they want to waterboard someone!

We have to beat them. It won't be easy. They have the power and ability to intimidate and deceive millions. This fight is not just between Democrats and Republicans. True, the Republican Party has been commandeered by corporate powers, but the Democratic Party has at least been infiltrated. Big money—and the politicians who are swayed by it—play both parties against each other, using this false battle to distract most of us from the real war, which is a war against the American family. For thirty years, starting with Ronald Reagan's presidency, the biggest heist in history has been going on right under our noses: an unprecedented transfer of wealth from the American middle class into the pockets of the super wealthy. In Eisenhower's day, the very rich paid 90 percent of their income in taxes. Today who bears the big tax burden? Everyday wage earners. And take a look at the last thirty years: In 1976, the top 1 percent of Americans earned 8.9 percent of the income; by 2005, they earned 21.8 percent. From 1979 to 2005, incomes for the top 5 percent increased 81 percent while incomes for the bottom 20 percent, the American workers, declined 1 percent. And as for net worth? As Inequality.org puts it, "The richest one percent of U.S. households now owns 34.3 percent of the nation's private wealth, more than the combined wealth of the bottom 90 percent."

Through jingoism, through attempts to rewrite history, through propaganda and by playing on people's coarsest emotions and fears, generations of right wing extremists have convinced the vast majority of Americans to vote against their own good. For three decades, a whole bunch of people, especially people in red states, people living paycheck to paycheck, voted for a criminal class who was stealing them blind. I guess we should be grateful the Republicans didn't legislate for debtor's prisons. A small percentage of moneyed elites have found a way to hold the rest of us financially hostage—and, as a country, we keep voting them and their henchmen into power. I'd call it Stockholm syndrome, but I can't because we're not in Sweden. You'd know if it were Sweden because we'd all have health care and a higher standard of living.

And I would be a better skier.

There's a saying where I come from: "You can lead a horse to water, but you can't get the dumb bastard to vote in his own interest." OK, maybe that saying has been heard only in my immediate family, but it's still worth saying because it's what happened.

THIS BATTLE HAS JUST BEGUN

In the year just past, the year of the Great Recession, there's been a glimmer of an awakening. Americans are mad as hell that they were forced to bail out crooked Wall Street institutions that were "too big to fail." Our government privatized corporate/banker profits and socialized corporate/banker losses, passing them right along to us. But a lot of this teabagger anger is misplaced. Bush and Cheney pulled the bank job and left Obama holding the bag—with nothing in it but an $11 trillion I.O.U. Some Americans have short-term memory issues. They forget that Obama and his much-maligned economic team did enough things right to save the economy from a total meltdown.

I have done my fair share of criticizing the Obama administration. Financial reform has been slow in coming, and the bonuses paid to the executives who have been bailed out are an outrage. But even though the White House spent too much time and money on Wall Street and not enough on Main Street, they got more right than they got wrong.

In the process, though, many of us have discovered that it is relatively easy to rally support in Washington if it helps out corporations, but any legislation designed to give the average American family a break results in instant gridlock: What the election of Barack Obama and a Democratic majority has revealed, plain as day, is just how entrenched and powerful big money interests have become. A few months into the

Obama presidency I began to understand that no matter how transformational this election was, it was not the end of the fight. It was just the beginning.

We voted for change, but not much changed. Dark forces still lurk. Big money still rules and big money still *makes* the rules. Senator Dick Durbin (D-IL) said on my show once, "The senate is owned by the banks." Or, you could say, it is co-owned by banks, the health care industry, and the oil monopolies. All that big money isn't going down soon and it isn't going down easy. Corruption is entangled in the system with cancerous tentacles. We can fight it and win, but it will be a fight that may well last generations.

If we fail, we could easily end up with these three classes—the rich, the struggling, and the poor. The sainted middle class? A memory, a ghost, a shadow. Gone. Sold down the river by greed. That's where we're headed, folks. *Compassion?* It's been moved to the back of the dictionary under S for shit out of luck.

To succeed, we have to reach back and rediscover our greatness. Tom Brokaw had it right when he called our parents and grandparents the Greatest Generation, because it was a generation that understood selflessness and sacrifice. What has the Me Generation sacrificed? Not much. This has been the greediest generation of Americans ever. And what are we leaving behind for the next generation? Debt. Corruption. Pollution. War. Can we allow that to be our legacy to our children and grandchildren?

We can blame our government and we can blame our political opponents, but in the end we can bring about change only if we are willing to change ourselves and the way we think. If we sit around waiting for someone to get it done, it won't get done. If we thought one campaign would turn it around, we now know that it won't.

"The standard answer is that we need better leaders. The real answer is that we need better citizens," wrote Thomas Friedman in one of his *New York Times* op-ed columns in fall 2009. "We need citizens who will convey to their leaders that they are ready to sacrifice, even pay, yes, higher taxes, and will not punish politicians who ask them to do the hard things."

Sacrifice is an interesting word. Life requires some sacrifices, and those who are unwilling to sacrifice find themselves paying dearly in the end. You pay now or you pay later with interest.

I always knew when I was playing football that all those wind sprints we suffered through in August's sweltering heat would pay off when our superior conditioning helped us win a tight game in October. But what I viewed then as a sacrifice, I realize now was an *investment,* and that's what I mean by changing the way we think. We need to be able to see past false choices. Doing the right thing *and* doing the fiscally responsible thing are often one and the same.

With an investment in universal health care we can put American businesses back on a level playing field with international competitors. Our investment will come back to us with a reduced trade deficit, more jobs, and a healthier workforce.

You want energy independence from our colluding faux friends in OPEC (the Organization of Petroleum Exporting Countries)? Let's invest in green energy now, and we won't be so inclined to send troops into the Middle East in the future. Our environment will be better for it.

We all know that a well-educated population makes for a stronger economy and a more vibrant democracy. It's one of Big Ed's Four Pillars of a great nation (something I cover in one of the key chapters of this book). Let's invest in our people. No one should be denied the opportunity to learn. How many potential Einsteins and Edisons are we leaving behind?

We're better than that. I know we are. I travel the country to town hall meetings hoping to inspire people with the hope I have for the future. But you know what? At every town hall, I find the people who show up, packed houses of them; they inspire me.

One day Wendy and I got into a taxi after a very hard day. The driver looked back in the mirror and recognized me. There was a pause and then he spoke softly. "Big Eddie. You're the one speaking the truth. You're the only one." That's all he said—but he touched my heart and lifted me up when I was a little down.

Most people have their heads and hearts in the right place, but we need a vision and a plan, too. There is a saying among pilots that you have to "fly ahead of the airplane." In other words, you have to understand where you are and anticipate the dangers ahead. That's what this book is about.

We'll get better government by being better citizens. The change starts when all of us are better informed and have the courage to share what we know. I believe most Americans stand on common ground, and if we demand that our elected leaders become more accountable to us, we can compromise and set aside wedge issues that are used to divide and conquer the American electorate.

I'm going to take on some other tough topics in this book, too, like immigration, tax policy, China's bid for economic supremacy, and the media. I've given these issues a great deal of thought and have offered some solutions in each chapter. You may have better ones. Super. Call my radio show (1-800-WE GOT ED) and let's talk. You may disagree. Fine. The open microphone is democracy in action, and your voice is crucial. As long as we have debate in this country, the truth will win out.

This is no time for complacency. Believe me when I say that you can make a difference. This is it, folks . . . the moment of truth. The American people voted for change, and now we will see if this is still a democracy or if big money has actually bought and sold everyone in Washington who can make a difference. This is a fight to see who is in charge of this nation, and the early returns are not good: *It ain't us.* This will be the moment historians will look back upon and either say it was the moment this great ship of state corrected its course, or the moment it sailed completely away from its democratic ideals.

CHAPTER ONE

FROM FARGO TO 30 ROCK

The Big Ed Story

PINCH ME. SERIOUSLY. I SEE THE FIRST RAYS OF DAWN RISING OVER the Hudson River, and I am twenty-seven floors up—at the top of the world really—and looking down at New York City. After I shower and shave, Wendy and I will take a short taxi ride to NBC Studios—30 Rock, home of MSNBC, from where the broadcast of *The Ed Show* originates. The place *Saturday Night Live* calls home. Legends have walked these halls. Legends still do. Me? I'm still new around here. I still look around with a real sense of wonder and a great appreciation for where I am, how far I've come, and who I've become.

You may know me as that guy from North Dakota because that's where I built my career, first as a television sportscaster and then as a regional radio talk-show host at one of the truly great radio stations in America, KFGO in Fargo. When we launched my national radio show, I took great pride in launching it from North Dakota.

Eric Sevareid, who came from North Dakota, once said the state was "a rectangular-shaped blank spot on the nation's consciousness," and I think North Dakotans are a little sensitive about that. This beautiful state and its beautiful people take tremendous pride in hometown boys and girls like Roger Maris, Peggy Lee, Angie Dickinson, Phil Jackson, Louis L'Amour, Lawrence Welk, and others who "made good."

Like Teddy Roosevelt, who ranched in the spectacular Badlands and fell in love with the place, I did, too, and was molded by the people and my experiences in North Dakota. We have a small getaway in Mott, in the southwestern part of the state, where pheasant and deer are plentiful. It helps me stay in touch with my adopted home.

ECHOES OF MY PAST

I grew up in Norfolk, Virginia, in a middle-class household. My dad was an aeronautical engineer for the government—and my mother was an English teacher who might well have been horrified by my occasional abuse of the rules of grammar in this book. They're both gone now, but when I look in the mirror I catch glimpses of them in myself. You know, I think the Lord only gives us two parents because we could never go through the loss of a third. After they were both gone, I felt like an orphan.

I hear their voices in mine from time to time, and I realize that many of my values are things they held dear. When I am faced with a tough decision, I still think about them and what I think they would do. You realize as the years pass how much of them is in you, and it makes you want to do as well for your own children.

Only time and experience can open your eyes to the importance of family as a stabilizing and guiding force in your life. I had terrific parents, and I didn't experience the generational schism so many parents and teens wrestled with in those days. Their values became my values. Their work ethic and sense of patriotism became mine. I grew up with a sense that I was required to make a difference.

Even when he was in his eighties, my father was thinking about and promoting energy independence. He was a patriot—loved his country—and he was so ethically grounded. In the 1980s, when executive pay began spiraling to obscene levels while the workingman was left behind, I remember my father saying, "I wonder how they sleep at night."

The times I grew up in shaped me, too. Like all teenagers in those days, I lived with the cloud of Vietnam hanging over my head, wondering if I would be drafted, wondering about the morality of the war itself.

My little league football coach Bill Bazmore died in Vietnam, and it profoundly affected me. He had always seemed *so old* to me, but a few years ago when Wendy and I found his name on the Vietnam War Memorial in Washington, D.C., I discovered he was just twenty-one when he died. Not many high school freshmen go to funerals, but I went to that one. It was a sobering experience, and I think that's part of the reason I became such an advocate for veterans. They are true champions for America.

I grew up aware of the civil rights movement and experienced the changes it brought about when I was bused to the slums of Norfolk, to a black school of eighteen hundred students. And *that* changed my life. While I was a minority there, no one made me feel like one. When I was just the third-string quarterback, my backfield coach, Joe Thornton, put a sign on my locker that still inspires me today: "Hustle is the Key to Survival."

By the time I was a senior in 1972, I was the starting quarterback and a team captain. My friends and teammates were black, but the only color that counted was the color of our jerseys. We trusted and loved one another like brothers. I cherish the memories and friendships from those days.

FROM NORFOLK TO FARGO-MOORHEAD

What I learned in Norfolk allowed me to play college ball for Moorhead State University, in Minnesota, which was just across the river from Fargo.

I led the nation in passing one year, but local sportscasters—one in particular, Jim Adelson—discovered I could talk a pretty good game, too. Adelson was a real showman and loved me because I was brash, and he loved a good controversy! He also took me under his wing and urged me to consider broadcasting as a career.

Of course, I had other dreams . . .

My senior year, NFL scouts began to show enough interest to give me hope. Former Green Bay Packers quarterback Zeke Bratkowski put me through a pretty good workout and was impressed. I could throw the ball. The Packers hinted that I might be taken in the third or fourth round of the 1978 draft, but it didn't happen that way. They poured salt into the wound by calling me during the eighth round to tell me that they wouldn't be drafting me and that no one else would be either, but they did want to sign me as a free agent. It was business, I realized later. Nothing personal.

But I was young and my pride was hurt, so I told them to kiss off. How many people get the chance to sign with the Green Bay Packers even as a free agent? Yeah, I probably made a mistake. Pride goeth before a fall. No shit-eth! I was devastated, but that was just one of the hard knocks and setbacks anyone experiences in life. My coach Ross Fortier kindly pulled a few strings and got me a tryout with John Madden and the Oakland Raiders, but I wasn't a good fit, and I got cut without playing a down. I was always grateful, though, for what Ross did for me.

Ross Fortier has been more than my coach. He has been like a father to me, especially after my own father died in 1992. Time and time again, the best advice I ever got was from Ross. What is it about guys who spend some time in life sweating together for a common goal? I guess that residual of hard work and effort never leaves you.

I think about my lost sports career from time to time. I would have been a good fit for the Packers, and I think I was as good as the guys they had that year, and maybe better, but that's life, isn't it? How can I regret the decisions I've made when I see all the wonderful places they have taken me?

I built a solid career in Fargo both in sportscasting and in conservative talk radio. Yes, I said conservative. I don't think I realized it then, but in some ways I had blinders on.

WENDY CHANGES MY LIFE

After I met Wendy, my blinders began to fall away. Man, she was something and still is. She's beautiful, super smart, and the kindest person I know. She's also a trained psychiatric nurse, which has its obvious advantages! For our first date, Wendy asked me to meet her at a homeless shelter where she volunteered. *A homeless shelter?* It hadn't really dawned on me that homelessness could exist in Fargo.

In my mind, a homeless person was a slacker, someone who just wasn't trying hard enough, and I said these self-righteous things on the air. I didn't know then that one in four homeless people is a Vietnam veteran.

At the shelter, some of the homeless welcomed me like a hero, a long-lost brother, and I began to feel ashamed of the things I had said. They patted me on the back, shook my hand. "You're the man, Big Ed," they said. Yeah, but why did I suddenly feel so small?

I fell in love with Wendy over a baloney sandwich on dry bread. She sparked an awakening, a new awareness in me that I didn't see coming. You don't know how narrow your vision has been until something or someone opens your eyes. I like to think she raised up the better angels within me. I don't think I was a bad person before and I don't presume to have become Mother Teresa since, but I'm a better person who thinks every day about being a better man. It's not like I was bathed in a heavenly light with the angels singing. I evolved. I guess I'm a Darwinian. I'm still a hard-driving competitor, but I think Wendy's influence helped me channel that energy in more positive ways. I can't imagine how much patience and understanding it took for Wendy to understand the "inner Ed."

THINKING FOR MYSELF

After I "came out" as a progressive, conservatives scoffed and branded me an opportunist. An opportunist in a nation where conservative voices dominated radio nine to one? I guess I was an opportunist with a poor grasp of the odds. Meanwhile, some liberals viewed me with suspicion because on some issues I just wasn't liberal enough. Here's the deal with me. I don't march in lockstep with any party line quite simply because I don't believe in everything each party stands for. I'll take my politics à la carte, please. I'm about the truth. It's just not in me to support something I don't believe in.

About the time I met Wendy, there was an epidemic of farm foreclosures across the Midwest, and as I spoke with those good people who were being run off the land after generations, it became clear to me that as a Republican, I had been on the wrong side of some issues. I just could not live in a sink-or-swim world, especially when it became clear that the game had been so egregiously fixed, that many hardworking Americans were being driven into poverty through no fault of their own. Maybe it was a combination of a rigged game and a little bad luck—a hailstorm or a drought—that did them in, but I knew unfairness when I saw it.

As an enthusiastic capitalist, I have worked hard to succeed. But I also realize that I caught a few breaks along the way. And I recognized over time that some people were being left behind. Capitalism allows innovators to innovate, and it works—with rules in place—but we ought not to get too enamored of the "purity" of any one system. Socialism, in the right measure, has some advantages, too. A blend of the two is what works best. Getting the balance right—that's what the big fight in the halls of commerce, er . . . *Congress* is all about.

I travel more than any talk-show host out there because I want to see for myself the way things are. Otherwise, it's easy to paint with a broad brush. And I take my shows on the road to address the issues from the places impacted by them.

I broadcast from Cuba during a trade mission. When the western Dakotas were in the midst of drought, we went on the road with truckloads of food and reported the sad fact that the proud farmers and ranchers could not afford to feed themselves. After Hurricane Katrina, *The Ed Schultz Show* went to New Orleans and helped relocate a couple of families to North Dakota to get back on their feet again. And I was in Washington, D.C., on September 11, 2001, in support of the nation's farmers who were lobbying for a better farm bill. Yes, I was in North Dakota senator Kent Conrad's office when the World Trade Center and then the Pentagon were hit, and I remember Laurie Boeder, the senator's communications director, saying, "This changes everything." My, how it did. Can you imagine being evacuated from the Hart Senate Building in Washington, D.C., in the United States of America? America lost her innocence that day.

Like most Americans, I supported President Bush during the crisis. I wanted very badly for him to succeed. In time, though, like so many other Americans, I lost faith in him and his administration. It became clear to me that they were leveraging the events of 9/11 for political gain. They were manipulating public fear to advance a private agenda and expand their political power. What they did was blatant, arrogant, and had nothing to do with democracy. With W in charge, the country was careening away from its ideals. The world that supported us on September 12, 2001, soon became disenchanted and frightened by the Bush administration's hubris and soon began to see George W. Bush as the most dangerous man on the planet. Sadly, so did many Americans. But publicly spoken opposition was too soft and came too late.

Even as I embraced the progressive movement in this country, I became frustrated by a lack of aggressiveness against an administration that seemed willing to shred the Constitution. The propaganda of right wing radio and Fox News was steering the country in the wrong direction. The docile mainstream media was letting them do it. And it was costing the Democrats elections.

I shared my opinions on this with the Democratic Caucus in Washington three times—once in 2002 and twice in 2003—and I told them point-blank, "You are not going to win unless you challenge the Right Wing Sound Machine."

DREAMING BIG: THE SHOW GOES NATIONAL

After I spoke to the Democratic Caucus in the fall of 2003, I received encouragement from my North Dakota senators, Kent Conrad and Byron Dorgan, as well as from Tom Daschle (D-SD), Harry Reid (D-NV), Deb Stabenow (D-MI), and Hillary Clinton (D-NY) to go ahead and fight back on the airwaves myself—with my own progressive radio program. And I had pretty much decided to do it.

"Ed, do you really think you can do this?" Hillary asked, and when I told her I thought it was possible, she said, "I'd like to help—I'll do anything to help."

"Well, you could be a guest on the show . . ."

And true to her word, she was. She's a great lady and a tremendous secretary of state.

As soon as Wendy and I started planning, the wheels began to turn, and a group called Democracy Radio, a nonprofit 501(c)(3), invested $1.8 million in seed money to launch the show. We had two years to make or break it, and the conventional wisdom in the business was that progressive radio didn't stand a chance.

When we launched with just two stations and me spouting blood from my nostrils, I wondered what the hell I had gotten myself into. There were days that the shows seemed endless because there were so few callers, and unlike other shows where the talkers pontificate and like to hear themselves talk, *The Ed Schultz Show* has always been caller driven. I go easy on the sermons. The callers make the show.

We needed advertisers even more. Again, the critics and the know-it-alls didn't believe we would find the support to survive. If pride has caused me to burn a few bridges in my time, it has also served me well at times like this. I got pissed at the very idea of failure. And when I was done being pissed, I got more resolute than I had ever been. If there is one thing I want to leave the kids, it's the memory that their dad never backed down, never gave up.

The number of callers increased and so did my audience. Advertisers soon discovered our show was an effective marketing tool. Because I know what it is like to build a business, I have a real admiration for small businesspersons. On Fridays for an hour, we do some "recession busting" by opening the lines to let entrepreneurs promote their businesses on nationwide radio. No charge. It started out as just something to do on a slow Friday, but it has grown into something I am quite proud of. We have helped businesses grow.

By the end of the first year of the national show, we had seventy stations. It was an incredible accomplishment for Team Fargo. But we were out of money. So I took out $600,000 in loans to keep the dream alive. Skin in the game, they call it.

By 2006, we had one hundred stations, and we were beginning to have an effect on the national discourse. You could feel the change in the air. Air America Radio, which launched shortly after I did, was out there, too, and my show was carried on many Air America stations. Suddenly, there were voices from the left being heard! Finally, someone was questioning the misinformation and propaganda coming from the Bush administration and their media supporters. I *know* we made a difference.

As the visibility of *The Ed Schultz Show* grew, we began to get calls from the cable networks for my commentary. As it turned out, having a bare-knuckle liberal brawler on the air to mix it up with the right wing ideologues was good for the ratings.

I was different from the liberals people were used to seeing on the air. Many of them were stereotypical geeky academic vegans with pocket protectors, bad hair, and Earth Shoes. I'm six-two, 250 pounds, and in a suit I would fit in on Wall Street. But I have a blue-collar soul. I'm a gun-toting, meat-eating, beer-drinking jockstrap. I remember one woman e-mailed C-SPAN during one of my early TV appearances. "You look like a conservative, you sound like a conservative . . . but the words are different!" I *am* different. The beautiful thing about the progressive movement is we have a big tent. I know I may not fit in a perfect liberal mold, but I don't think anyone ought to have to pass a political purity test to be on my team.

If I can point to one gift the good Lord has given me, it is my ability to think quickly on my feet. Not everyone has it. That's why most talk shows don't like the unpredictability of unscreened callers. I love the challenge. I know what I believe, but it isn't about always being right. It's about the free and open debate. Sometimes callers change my mind. That kind of talk radio honed my skills and made me very effective on cable television. Eventually, Wendy and I had to invest in a satellite up-link so we could be available when the shows called. I began to think, "Hey, I can make a success out of this." We started talking seriously about a television show.

A TURNING POINT

A pivotal moment for *The Ed Schultz Show* happened in 2008 when Barack Obama made a campaign visit to Grand Forks, North Dakota. I have long been an admirer of Hillary Clinton, but after meeting Obama in Washington, I was so impressed, I became convinced he was the right person at the right time to become president. Though I have been critical of him sometimes, I still believe that.

During Obama's visit to North Dakota, I was asked to warm up a huge stadium crowd. Now, anyone that has ever heard me speak knows I have one temperature and one speed—hot and full steam ahead, and I don't mince words. I had become increasingly concerned about John McCain's hawkish stance during the campaign and the idea of four more years of a Bush-Cheney style approach to the two ongoing wars. Like I said, I'm not the kind of guy who minces words. I called McCain a warmonger. It wasn't the first time, but it was the first time network cameras were there.

Both the righties and the lefties went wild—for different reasons, of course. With the Right, it was pretty much "how dare you!" And from the Left, people were just glad someone had the guts to say it. In many ways, John McCain has been a political sacred cow because of his military service and because he's a pretty good guy. There is much to admire. However, I think as a candidate he began to compromise his own values to get elected—imagine any politician doing that! In the end, I think it was a good thing to confront John McCain.

It also raised my visibility nationwide. Was this a calculated dustup on my part? Heck no! I just say what's on my mind and let the chips fall where they may. I never intended to grow up to be controversial, but I recognize now that I am.

GO EAST, YOUNG MAN!

After Obama won his historic election, I felt drawn to Washington, where the action was. This was history and I wanted to be a part of it. The country was at a crossroads. From a professional standpoint, I wanted to be more accessible to the talking-head shows, and then there was a dream . . . that my next step in fighting this fight would be a television show.

The plan was to do a [local] Sunday-morning show in Washington and grow it just like we had the national radio show. Sure, some of it was about building my career. I believe in "growing the brand." And like any man, I want to make sure my family is well provided for, but there was a larger purpose, too. I wanted my voice to be heard—I wanted to be a voice for change.

Unfortunately, we hit town in January 2009, just as the economy went into free fall; it was a terrible time to launch a show because people were so worried about the economy, our deal fell apart, and there we were, facing another roadblock. We lost $500,000 in advertising sponsorships almost overnight. It's hard to tell you just how devastating it was—and just how uncertain our lives had become. We had moved to Washington, D.C., on a hope and a prayer, and it turned out, that's about all we had.

But my career has been built with what some would call gambles and what I call faith. A friend told me later, angels ride on the shoulders of the bold.

We lost the TV show on Friday.

On Monday, I got a call from MSNBC.

Phil Griffin wanted to meet me. Phil had become president of MSNBC in July 2008 after building an impressive résumé in other positions with NBC and MSNBC. He had been with MSNBC since its launch in 2006 and had helped put together a remarkable stable of talent.

In Phil Griffin I met my match and then some. This guy has more passion than I do—which is a little like calling the pope an agnostic. I was intense, focused, and ready to grab Phil by the throat and make him give me the job. He was equally intense, and his competitive spirit made me feel right at home. Well, a twenty-minute cup of coffee in a small café in a Washington hotel with Phil Griffin turned into two hours.

Wendy was waiting patiently outside for me in the hotel lobby when I finally emerged. She knew the length of the meeting was a good sign. I'll never forget that we both had tears in our eyes. The first thing I said to Wendy was "I think this guy is going to hire me," and we hugged each other like we were never going to let go. This was it. I was going to get my chance at TV.

Not long afterward I found myself substitute-hosting the program *1600 Pennsylvania Avenue.* After the third audition, Phil Griffin said, "You're hired," and he encouraged Wendy and me to move to Manhattan.

Can you imagine? You're talking about a guy who has a lake home in Minnesota so he can fish at a moment's notice. Now we would be living just a few blocks from 30 Rock, one of the most famous showbiz addresses in the world. I could not believe all of this was happening.

Sometimes hopes and prayers can be pretty powerful.

For five and a half years all we had ever heard was that progressive talk couldn't make it and that we could never make it to the next level. You don't just go from Fargo to 30 Rock . . . but *we* were on our way. We had our shot.

I remember thinking, "Holy cow! The kids are gonna think we're crazy." We'd be leaving the lake country in Minnesota (fifty miles east of Fargo is where we live) for the big city and a small apartment, along with a hope and a prayer. None of our six kids—they're all adults now—could believe what was going on. They were all genuinely excited and happy for us. They knew how badly I wanted this.

I don't know if Megan, Christian, Joe, Greta, Ingrid (Wendy's kids from a previous marriage), and David (my son from a previous marriage) know how much they have influenced the way I view the world. They're all in their twenties, smart and thoughtful. They inspire me and motivate me to do what I can to leave them a better world.

Christian and Joe have been in my life for thirteen years and are my partners in E. A. Schultz Construction. They are tough, hardworking, and loyal men. The girls, Megan, Greta, and Ingrid, are all married with children. They are great moms married to solid men whom I trust—even when the fishing and hunting stories start flying around the room. My son Dave is a professional golfer. We all live and die with every putt.

Our Minnesota lake home is where everyone comes together during the holidays. At Thanksgiving, we set the table for thirty-four! I call the family the Brady Bunch on steroids, but when we all get together with Buck, our beloved black Lab, playing gently with the kids by the fireplace, the gang has a Norman Rockwell feel to it.

GROWING PAINS

Although I had done many appearances on talking-head shows, I had not done television full-time since 1996 when I had been a Fargo sportscaster, so it took awhile to get my sea legs on *The Ed Show*. Any new show has its growing pains as the team learns to work together. I was surrounded by professionals, and that was a comfort, but internally I struggled for the first two months. I wanted so badly to succeed I think at times I tried too hard. Sometimes I get so focused I forget to enjoy the experience! I don't care what it is, a town hall meeting, a Ladies Aid meeting, or a national TV broadcast, I prepare the same way I did for football games. I start to tune out everything before I go on. *Focus. Focus.*

In time I began to reach a comfort level—something that comes only when you begin to trust your team and they begin to have more confidence in you. Some days it felt so good, I didn't want the show to end. One day, after a really good show, I told a friend of mine on the phone, "Man, I have an idea how a junkie feels. This could be addictive." There's no better feeling than hitting it out of the park. It's like putting on the pads for a big game.

I remain grateful for Phil Griffin's patience as we went through our early growing pains. I was glad we could reward him with the best numbers MSNBC had recorded in that time slot—ever. Having 3.5 million radio listeners made a big difference because I was able to cross-promote the shows. If we can register the same solid, steady growth with the TV show as we have with the radio program, we'll have a good run. Make no mistake; it is all about the numbers in this business. The overnight ratings come out every day at 4 P.M. You live day to day for the first few years in this business. You have to be a realist. The life expectancy of most shows on television is short.

The first *Ed Show* was broadcast at 6 P.M. on April 7, 2009. In order to make room for *The Ed Show,* David Shuster, an Emmy award–winning broadcaster, got bumped from the time slot. David has been an absolute pro—very gracious. I've experienced a few knocks in my life, and I greatly respected the way David handled this one. He's a talented journalist and an even better person, a real stand-up guy. He continues to work at MSNBC as an anchor and correspondent.

I never imagined I would be standing on a stage quite so large, able to reach so many people. It's both humbling and an awesome responsibility. But without meaning to sound grandiose, I believe this is what I was born to do. After every show Wendy and I go back to the apartment in New York to watch the show on TiVo, just to make sure this really happened today . . . are we really doing this?

CHAPTER TWO

THE FOUR PILLARS

Let's Fly Ahead of the Plane

AS COMPLEX AS ANY NATION MIGHT BE, I BELIEVE THERE ARE SIMPLE, essential components to a great country. I call them the Four Pillars. If you have been a listener of *The Ed Schultz Show* or read my first book, *Straight Talk from the Heartland,* you may be familiar with my concept. Since they are such critical elements of a great nation and a vibrant middle class, it's important we start this with an overview of these pillars:

I.   Defend the Nation
II. Establish a Sound Fiscal Policy
III. Feed the Country
IV. Educate the People

A country that can successfully do these things will prosper. Weakness in any one of these areas is like a hole in the dike: In time, you're going to be under water.

The interesting thing about the American democracy, with all its checks and balances and built-in gridlock, is that it often takes a crisis of some sort—typically economic or military—before the country wakes up and is ready to make the changes necessary to fortify these pillars. The bigger the crisis, the more likely it is that the nation will get to work.

Barack Obama seems to understand this as well as anyone since Franklin Roosevelt. Take the economic crisis of 2008–2009, for instance. A healthy economy is all about confidence, and both FDR and Obama understood they had to reassure everyone on a national level that the banking system wouldn't completely fail.

Just before Roosevelt took office in 1933, a nationwide banking crisis began to boil. Interestingly, Herbert Hoover reached out as a lame duck president to President-elect Roosevelt to issue a joint statement support-ing a bank holiday, an offer Roosevelt declined, choosing, apparently, to keep all the credit (or blame) to himself. Once in office, he announced a bank holiday so banks could be inspected and declared solvent or shut down. As you can imagine, when those banks reopened with this gov-ernment stamp of approval, citizens had much more faith in them.

In the biggest economic meltdown of our own time, most econo-mists credit the Troubled Assets Relief Program (TARP), which was introduced in September 2008, with keeping the country and the world out of a full-blown depression. Remember, this crisis took place late in Bush 43's second term, but he and President-elect Obama, perhaps learning from history, worked together, which helped steady the econ-omy. One could make the case that from the start, Obama chose to do what was better for the country rather than choosing to cynically and politically let Bush go down with the ship as Roosevelt had let Herbert Hoover do.

The full effects of the Obama Stimulus Package, which involves a combination of tax breaks for individuals; state and local government relief; infrastructure, antipoverty, health care, education, and energy mea-sures, will not be felt until 2011, but the confidence it and other measures gave us all in the short run was critical to stabilizing the economy.

The Cash for Clunkers program provided a shot in the arm to auto-makers and their suppliers. Critics don't realize that by stepping in to bail out GM and Chrysler, Obama probably saved Ford and a multitude of parts suppliers that supply the Big Three. Had Chrysler and GM failed, it would have killed many of the suppliers that sell to Ford, and Ford almost certainly would have come crashing down, too.

Confidence is not something that is easily measurable, so critics have been able to Monday-morning quarterback the Obama administration on any number of issues—including joblessness and a rising deficit—but things would have been much, much worse had he not acted so decisively.

By December 2009, job losses—eleven thousand—were the lowest in two years, signaling the "beginning of the end" of the recession. Auto sales and retail sales were up. Housing sales grew dramatically in October 2009, spurred in part by an $8,000 tax credit for first-time home buyers.

So in the short term Obama took strong steps to point this country in the right direction. However, each step has been an excruciatingly slow process. Much of the problem has been Republican obstructionists in the Senate who drag out each bill and amendment—a stall tactic to keep Democratic reforms off the table as long as possible.

Imagine Obama as a schoolboy pulling a little blue wagon filled with playmates to school. If half of the passengers drag their feet, it will be slow going and they will be late. Naturally, they will blame Obama. That's what he is up against in the Senate.

However, a bill passed in the House in December 2009 (it will need to pass the Senate and be signed by the president to become law) offers hope. The bill seeks oversight of institutions "too big to fail," creates a consumer financial protection agency to prevent risky lending practices like those in the real estate sector that triggered the Great Recession, gives shareholders a vote on executive compensation, regulates derivatives and hedge funds, and opens the books of the Federal Reserve.

If you listen carefully in the wind, you can hear screaming on Wall Street. But Obama's reforms come from the FDR playbook, which many historians and economists credit with preserving the stability and integrity of the economy for fifty years. Senator Byron Dorgan (D-ND) warned in 1999 as he opposed sweeping rollbacks of FDR-era regulations, "I think in 10 years time we will look back and say, 'We should not have done that,' because we forgot the lessons of the past." How prophetic he proved to be.

OPPORTUNITY BORN OF CRISIS

Thinking longer term and thinking about leveling the playing field are keys to what FDR did. Recognizing that the economic crisis that was the Great Depression had a twin—economic *opportunity*—he set in motion changes that helped create a half century of unprecedented prosperity. By encouraging unions and then in 1944 establishing the G.I. Bill, Roosevelt set in motion the rise of the middle class. Unions tempered the strength of corporations, and the G.I. Bill helped educate and/or finance the homes of 7.8 million World War II veterans.

Roosevelt wasn't just reacting to the immediate crisis when he created the Federal Deposit Insurance Corporation to instill confidence in depositors, or when he created Social Security to ease the stress of retirement, or created commodity safety nets to ensure cheap and abundant food. He was setting in motion policies that would transform the future. He was thinking ahead. All of this from a guy who was considered an intellectual lightweight.

FDR instinctively understood that greatness in America did not reside alone with the wealthy titans of industry, the aristocratic world in which he grew up, but in the middle class. Roosevelt understood at a gut level that given a fair shake, the common man would become the economic engine that would make America a superpower.

He could see generations ahead.

As a pilot, my life and the lives of my passengers depend on what is called "flying ahead of the plane"—that means anticipating problems and devising solutions before things get out of hand. Everybody knows where we *are*. The trick is to understand where we are *headed*, and that kind of thinking is typically lacking in democracies and capitalistic societies because politicians are thinking in two-, four-, and six-year election cycles and, even worse, CEOs are trying to keep stockholders happy from quarter to quarter.

Most of our lawmakers get too preoccupied with short-term success for themselves on Election Day to look ahead and do the right thing for our kids' future. Congress gets a world-class pension and world-class health care. Relative to most Americans, they live like rock stars. Not like Mick Jagger, but maybe like Milli Vanilli, and that ain't bad.

And as senators and congressmen approach another election, they start thinking long and hard about the short term—about how each vote might be used against them in the next election; then they do what's best for their reelection chances and not always what's good for the country in the long run. So each generation of leaders in government and business lives in the now and blithely ignores the future.

Every political party and every generation has done it, though none as spectacularly destructively as George W. Bush's administration. He took a debt that under Bill Clinton was theoretically on track to be paid off by now, and saddled us with an $11 trillion debt by insanely giving tax breaks to the rich and picking a $3 trillion fight with Iraq.

George W. Bush put us into a crisis situation. OK. What's the opportunity in this self-induced crisis? Well, to start with, we have to recalibrate our moral compass as a nation and ask ourselves, Are we so lacking in character that we will allow our children to pay for our mistakes?

The good news is that we do have the opportunity to do something about our national lack of foresight: We can do something about the national debt right now. The progressive movement has the House of Representatives, the White House, and a majority in the Senate. This chance reminds me of George C. Scott's quote from the movie *Patton:*

We have "precisely the right instrument, at precisely the right moment of history, in exactly the right place." What remains to be seen is whether we have the *will,* whether the Democrats can stick together, and find one Republican with a conscience, because if they don't, this rare opportunity to save our children's future will have been squandered.

I think in some ways President Obama's task is more difficult than Roosevelt's. FDR enjoyed a strong Democratic majority in Congress. And during World War II, Americans and Congress understood the threat from the Axis powers and were more willing to back the president. Today, the threat to America does not seem as immediate to a tragically uninformed American public. Most Americans have not connected the dots between the crushing debt and the resulting inability of the country to afford satisfactory health care and education for its citizens. Most Americans don't seem to understand that the American Dream is growing dim and the carcasses of the late, great middle class are being picked clean by corporate vultures in a class war dominated by the rich. Tragically, the neocon opposition is willing to undermine the presidency and drag the country down in an effort to regain power. It's a dangerous, unpatriotic, political game, but it is a game progressives and the middle class could win by being informed and by having the courage to tell the truth to others.

Let's think long term—as most of our elected leaders do not. Let's talk about the Four Pillars.

Pillar #1: Defend the Nation

I'm not a general and I'm not a diplomat, but I've read enough history to know that (1) as long as there are men with dark hearts, we have to be ready to fight them, and (2) war more often produces two losers than a winner and a loser.

Defending the nation takes a delicate balance. Reach too far, and eventually the nation begins to fall apart. Consider Rome, Great Britain, and the USSR—and the path America has been on for many years as the world's policeman. We need to look no further than Vietnam and Iraq before we see parallels with the superpowers of the past. While we have built a great military machine, we have shortchanged our citizens and ignored our infrastructure—and other nations have built up major economies.

In 2007, Representative Ron Paul, a doctor, a Republican congressman from Texas, and a two-time presidential candidate, told Maria Bartiromo for an article in *BusinessWeek*, "The easiest place to cut spending is overseas because it's doing so much harm to us, undermining our national defense and ruining our budget. I would start saving hundreds of billions of dollars by giving up on defending the American empire. . . . I'd start bringing our troops home, not only from the Middle East, but from Korea, Japan, and Europe, and save enough money to slash the deficit. We can actually pay down the national debt and still take care of people here at home."

When it comes to defending our nation, restraint is a good thing. As mighty as America is, we are not mighty enough to force our sense of morality or our system on the rest of the world. The reality is, you just can't take out every despot. When it comes to being commander in chief, pragmatism is a virtue.

Historically, America's leaders tend to be pragmatic, but, as in Vietnam, we are sometimes too slow to come to realize that there's nothing to be won. As Robert McNamara, JFK's defense secretary, discovered, the United States can fight any war to a *stalemate,* but victory can be all but unattainable in what are really civil wars, such as Vietnam and Korea. In Iraq, we discovered that once we had removed Saddam's iron grip, what was left were two distinctly warring factions—the Sunnis and the Shia—*and* the Kurds, an ethnic group of Sunnis.

The Bush administration didn't seem to have a clue that this would happen. They acted as if with Saddam Hussein gone, Iraq would unite, and they didn't plan for any other scenario. Nor did they have a plan for

Afghanistan. We have al-Qaeda on the defensive, and we ought to continue to relentlessly hunt Osama bin Laden until the day he dies, but occupying Afghanistan is a fool's errand, as the Soviet Union discovered two decades ago. We can win territory, but is it worth the price of holding it?

We should not have been surprised by the thirty-thousand-troop U.S. surge in Afghanistan, which Obama announced in December 2009: He is doing what he said he was going to do—draw down in Iraq and finish the job in Afghanistan with a strategy to occupy and stabilize population centers while training Afghans to defend their country, a strategy that seems to be working in Iraq. And we should be encouraged that NATO immediately added seven thousand troops from twenty-five countries to help.

In this instance, Obama's global popularity has paid big dividends. In a very diplomatic manner, Obama reminded the rest of the world that defeating al-Qaeda is in everyone's best interest. He has also wisely reframed this fight not as a war against terror but as a fight against al-Qaeda—the specific group that attacked us on 9/11. The president's eighteen-month timeline for success may prove to be too optimistic, but giving a timeline sends a message of urgency to the Afghanistan government and, let's face it, placates the left wing of the Democratic Party.

I applaud the president's pragmatism as he deals with the bad hand he was dealt by the Bush administration, and I took as a good sign his somber welcome at Dover Air Force Base in October 2009 of the bodies of eighteen soldiers slain in Afghanistan, something neither Bush nor Cheney ever did. President Obama saw the flag-draped caskets and the weeping families, and he needed to. Every president needs to feel that kind of pain. War should never be easy.

America lost more than 300 soldiers in Afghanistan in 2009, and has lost more than 900 total since the war began in 2001. More than 2,700 soldiers have been wounded (and not returned to duty), according to official military statistics. Some estimates place civilian deaths in Afghanistan well above 7,000.

Most Americans seem to believe that the fight against al-Qaeda in Afghanistan is necessary. Upon acceptance of his Nobel Peace Prize, President Obama said, "We must begin by acknowledging the hard truth that we will not eradicate violent conflict in our lifetimes. There will be times when nations—acting individually or in concert—will find the use of force not only necessary but morally justified."

However, I do not believe the preemptive war with Iraq was justi-fied. I think it was a blunder that set a dangerous modern-day precedent for preemptive war and seriously damaged U.S. credibility around the world—something only time and credible action in the future can miti-gate. History alone knows how this war will play out. What we can be certain about is that Bush's Iraq folly placed a tremendous financial bur-den on the nation that has critically weakened us both militarily and financially.

The number of American casualties in Iraq has surpassed the 2,973 killed on 9/11. The more than 4,300 casualties in Iraq may seem small by historic wartime benchmarks, but it's not a small number if you're the one visiting the grave on Memorial Day. Another 31,000 soldiers have been injured in Iraq. The civilian death toll in Iraq is an estimated 100,000.

THE OTHER BURDEN OF WAR

Along with the human cost, there's the financial burden of war—a bur-den that has human costs, too—in terms of higher taxes, lifelong debt for our children, and lost opportunity to rebuild infrastructure at home. War, first and foremost, is big business. America is the biggest arms dealer in the world. In 2009, the estimate of U.S. government arms sales was $40 billion, up from $32 billion in 2008. In the short term, selling arms builds relationships between America and our allies, like Israel, and keeps production lines moving, but the arms business is not always an efficient process. A 2008 *Washington Post* report said "the Govern-ment Accountability Office found that 95 major [military] systems have exceeded their original budgets by a total of $295 billion." Look, I know we need new technologies to simultaneously make our country more secure while keeping our soldiers safer, but I can give you 295 billion reasons we need to ratchet up the oversight.

How much of the 2010 projected $3.6 trillion national budget goes to military spending? According to the Department of Defense, about $670 billion, which includes $130 billion for Iraq—assuming the exit strategy goes according to plan. The price of "victory" is more than $10 billion a month!

If you add in military-related costs that fall outside the defense budget, the real total of the military expenditures is closer to $1 trillion a year. In any given recent year, the United States has accounted for about *half* of global military spending—six times as much as China and ten times as much as Russia.

According to a study by Joseph Stiglitz, a Nobel Prize–winning economist, and Linda Bilmes, an economist at Harvard University's Kennedy School of Government, the total estimated cost of the war when all is said and done will be $3 trillion. If you include Afghanistan and relatable costs to the economy, the total approaches $5 trillion!

Compare that to the cost of universal health care coverage over ten years—even the most extreme estimates have been around the $1 trillion mark. We could insure the next generation with what we have squandered in Iraq.

BIG OIL WEAKENS OUR DEFENSE

There are many things other than war that support or undermine a nation's ability to defend itself, some of which, like economic strength and an abundant food supply, will be more fully explored when we talk about the other three pillars. There are also national policies, including the way we approach energy consumption and procurement, that directly affect our national security, including the ways we deploy our troops.

I don't believe for a moment that we would focus on the desert sands of the Middle East the way we do if all that oil wasn't critical to our power.

In reality, our soldiers don't just protect against invasion at home, they protect our economic interests abroad. America imports some $300 billion in oil each year—20 to 25 percent from the Middle East—to keep the economy humming. (Close to 70 percent of all the oil we consume is imported.) So what you pay at the pump is much more than you think. Tesla Motors founder Elon Musk says the price of gas should probably be $10 per gallon, and I think he's in the ballpark. There's no line item breaking down the exact cost to us of subsidizing Big Oil, but a 2005 study by the International Center for Technology Assessment calculated the annual cost of U.S. military expenses related to protecting foreign oil for our use might approach $100 billion a year.

It's important to understand the hidden costs in oil because when it comes to energy independence, free market purists rail against subsidies for biofuels or other homegrown energy sources, like solar or wind technologies, without ever acknowledging that the existing system *already* dramatically subsidizes Big Oil. Keeping one or more of our eleven carrier groups parked in the Persian Gulf doesn't come cheap.

The point here is obvious. The less we depend on the rest of the world for energy, or *anything* for that matter, the less pressure we put on our military.

We should not shy away from subsidizing domestic energy to free us from dependence on foreign oil—starting with OPEC's oil. This outfit (the Organization of Petroleum Exporting Countries) has had us hamstrung for years. Let's find a way to stop doing business with them. Politically and militarily, that makes us more independent and stronger. Energy independence is a major step toward better defending the nation.

We need to phase out our use of petroleum-based fuels in favor of clean and renewable energy, like hydrogen, but we also need to recognize that there will be a long transition phase. Ethanol from corn may not be ideal, but it should be part of the transition until cellulose-based ethanol is fully developed. Synthetic fuels from coal should be part of that transition as well. Until these emerging fuels can stand on their own in the market-place, government subsidies almost certainly will be necessary. When the cost of these subsidies is debated, it will be important to remember that Big Oil is already being subsidized in dollars and in American blood.

THE PATRIOT ACT VS. THE CONSTITUTION

After 9/11, the Bush administration pulled the Patriot Act out of some neocon's drawer somewhere and shoved it down our throats. If you voted against it, the implication was you were soft on terrorism. With little debate and without many people even having read the law that granted sweeping new police powers and steamrolled right over the Constitu-tion, the Patriot Act was approved.

The Fourth Amendment to the Constitution guarantees that "the right of the people to be secure in their persons, houses, papers, and ef-fects, against unreasonable searches and seizures, shall not be violated, and no warrants shall issue, but upon probable cause. . . ." The Patriot Act violated the Fourth Amendment; it opened the door to warrantless wiretaps. In 2007, a federal judge struck down the part of the Patriot Act allowing the FBI to obtain e-mail and telephone data from private com-panies for counterterrorism investigations.

Still, because of this act, we may now have to redefine what an illegal search is and what the inevitable ramifications are of being searched. Do we want to live in a world in which every e-mail and every statement is analyzed to decide if we are an enemy of the state? Do we want our credit card purchases and library records examined by the government? Do we want them tracking us by our cell phones? What about facial-recognition software? It can be used to spot known terrorists in airports. But it could also to be used to track your every move. Your cell phone tells Big Brother every move you make.

"The Patriot Act's key provisions focus primarily on data collection. The underlying assumption is that the real problem here is a lack of information," said James Walsh, former executive director, Project on Managing the Atom/Science, Technology, and Public Policy Program, in an opinion piece in the *San Francisco Chronicle*. "The history of intelligence failures suggests, however, that often the problem is not a lack of data, but rather making sense of the data you already have. Sometimes it's the case of the left hand not knowing what the right hand has. After the 1993 bombing of the World Trade Center, the FBI discovered that it already had copies of maps and detailed plans of the attack before it happened."

After dissecting all the missed opportunities to thwart the plot to destroy the Twin Towers in 2001, it became obvious that turf battles between the FBI and CIA and other federal agencies were part of the problem. Even where there were no turf battles, there was no information shared. Had information been shared and proper procedures followed, most of the hijackers would never have been allowed to board. Once they were aboard, the communication between the FAA and the military was so slow, an effective defense—which would have meant shooting down passenger jets—could not be mounted. Communication between President Bush and the White House could not be established for some time during the crisis. In short, the intelligence part of our defense system failed.

Before 9/11, the Bush administration had many pieces of the terror plot puzzle sitting right in front of them, but they were unable to put them together in time. British Intelligence had warned two years earlier that planes might be used to attack American targets. The Bush administration knew this. By the summer of 2001, elements of the government knew a terrorist attempt by al-Qaeda was about to happen. The president even received a memo while on vacation in Texas about bin Laden's determination to attack within the United States. But no action was taken. If you had reliable intelligence that terrorists were going to attack within the United States, wouldn't you at least increase security at airports? Wouldn't you advise the FAA, the military?

Despite his warnings to the incoming president, Bill Clinton bears responsibility, too. After the 1993 bombing of the World Trade Center, the terrorists were brought to justice, but an examination of the holes in national security should have ended the turf wars and improved information sharing between agencies like the FBI and the CIA. You can't put the puzzle together if people are hoarding some of the pieces.

After a terrorist plot was uncovered and a suspect arrested in Denver in 2009, we learned that law enforcement agencies both domestic and international had been tracking those involved for two years. Najibullah Zazi, a native of Afghanistan, reportedly received training in al-Qaeda camps. That indicates a much more functional flow of information, *and* it suggests that good old-fashioned police work, properly authorized, is still the most effective defense against these criminals. Over the course of a two-year investigation, there is plenty of time to obtain proper search warrants.

THE PATRIOT ACT WAS AN OVERREACTION

We got a wake-up call in 1993, but when it came to improving the flow of information between law enforcement agencies, we didn't answer the call for eight more years, and when we did, we overreacted.

The Patriot Act was an overreaction.

Representative Ron Paul (R-TX) observed in 2005, after terrorist bombings in London, "Let's remember that London is the most heavily monitored city in the world, with surveillance cameras recording virtually all public activity in the city center. British police officials are not hampered by our Fourth Amendment nor by our numerous due process requirements. In other words, they can act without any constitutional restrictions, just as supporters of the Patriot Act want our own police to act. Despite this they were not able to prevent the bombings, proving that even a wholesale surveillance society cannot be made completely safe against determined terrorists. Congress misses the irony entirely. The London bombings don't prove the need for the Patriot Act, they prove the folly of it. . . . Most governments, including our own, tend to do what they can get away with rather than what the law allows them to do. All governments seek to increase their power over the people they govern, whether we want to recognize it or not. . . . Constitutions and laws don't keep government power in check; only a vigilant populace can do that."

What we don't know is what we don't know. What I mean by that is that only a select few high-ranking government officials have an idea of the methods being used to gather information and how much directly violates the Constitution. Nor do we have any idea how much information is being gathered on the Internet, through eavesdropping, or even from spy satellites, and how much of it is valuable in the fight against terrorism. Nor do we know how much of it has the potential to be used for political purposes—and that is where the danger lies.

Somebody, please convince me that there is enough oversight in these matters!

Why did we let the Patriot Act happen? It all comes down to fear. If our government can keep us fearful, as the Bush-Cheney administration did, we will lose sight of what it means to be Americans. But if we believe our ideals are too important to compromise for the momentary illusion of safety, if we can accept that the world is sometimes a dangerous place and choose to just keep living in spite of it, we will keep the flame of freedom alive.

Pillar #2: Establish a Sound Fiscal Policy

When, in the final days of his administration, President George W. Bush called on Congress to approve TARP (the Troubled Asset Relief Program), the elephantine $700 billion fund to steady the financial sector, I supported the bill. My gut and Senator Kent Conrad (D-ND) both told me that if we didn't rescue the banks from their own bad behavior, it would be catastrophic, affecting *everyone,* at every economic level.

Conrad put it this way: "The patient was on the table, we had to do something and fast." He acknowledged it was one of those deals where you operate with one hand and hold your nose with the other. When we secured all that bad debt, we *privatized* the profits of investment banks (the banks get to keep the profits) and *socialized* the losses (the American people get the losses).

An awful lot of true conservatives thought that we ought to let the banks go broke. As a former Republican and a guy who still likes a balanced checkbook, I was torn. But my instincts told me that the cost of bailing out these turkeys was less than letting them drag everyone else down, too. As it has played out, it seems these measures did save us from a far worse global meltdown.

However, Wall Street emerged as clueless and tone deaf as ever, lavishing extravagant pay on executives with government bailout money. The backlash hurt Democrats, and ironically so did efforts to oversee executive pay, which were seen as socialistic.

We were living in a pump-and-dump balloon economy, in which stocks and real estate are overvalued (and the crooks who set it up get out fast, just before a crash). And the dust hasn't settled yet. Plenty of smart people warned against rampant speculation in the housing market, and a whole lot of other smart people took advantage of it while the getting was good.

If you proposed the mortgage business model that American bankers were using before 2008 to any sane society, the people would either arrest you or drag you in for psychoanalysis. But here mortgage lenders earned *bonuses* for processing loans with escalating payments to people who could not afford the homes they were buying. (How is that not a crime?) In the days of old-fashioned banking, a banker was very motivated to do due diligence on his customers, because the bank's money was on the line. For the bank to survive, most of the loans had to be good. But under the rules of the game that created this recent debacle, lenders were able to make these bad loans, bundle them with others, and sell them with a bogus Triple A rating to investors.

And what agency in its right mind would rate these toxic assets Triple A? Oh, enablers like Moody's, Standard & Poor's, and Fitch, all of which profited immensely from this ratings charade. Meanwhile, banks no longer had to wait thirty years to profit from a mortgage. They got a quick, clean score, and passed the bad loan off down the line like a hot potato. With the quick return on their investment, banks were eager to make even more bad loans. By 2006, there were $2.5 trillion in mortgages floating around Wall Street, and no one could tell the good from the bad because, hell, they all had the gold seal of approval from rating institutions. The rating institutions "made the market. Nobody would have been able to sell these bonds without the ratings," Ohio attorney general Marc Dann told Jesse Eisinger for a piece in *Portfolio* magazine.

These false mortage ratings drove up real estate buying and artificially increased home values, so Americans did what they foolishly had been told was acceptable—they used the roof over their heads as collateral for more loans and for unsustainable consumer spending. Dumb. Instead of treating our homes as sanctuaries, we treated them as banks. There was greed on Wall Street and naïveté and ignorance in the suburbs.

This is the bad behavior we bailed out. You bet it was a tough pill to swallow. But my hope is that eventually, the market will recover and the American taxpayer will see a profit from the resale of these "toxic assets." I expect this recovery to be a measured one because there will be less consumer spending—the American consumer can't or won't go further into personal debt to bail out the economy this time—and in some respects that's actually good news because the result of this fiasco is that Americans have begun to reduce personal debt and save more. However, to keep the economy from stalling, the Obama administration was forced to do what FDR did: spend stimulus money. It's another bitter pill to swallow for a guy like me who hates too much debt, but I recognize that the cure is marginally less painful than the ailment.

Here's what is exasperating, though. George W. Bush ran up the debt to nosebleed levels. It really galls me to hear how Bush and Cheney made us safer! They left us with our asses hanging out in the wind is what they did. You can't have a strong country without a strong economy. They left us broke down and busted, critically weakened. They may as well have used all that red ink to paint a target on our backs. Bush and Cheney left Obama with no recourse other than to spend more to keep our economy moving. That is exactly what respected economists say must be done, even when deficit spending and lagging tax receipts have the country facing a trillion-dollar budget deficit for the first time in history.

Mark Thoma, an economist at the University of Oregon, expresses a common view on his personal website: "The question of how bad would economic conditions be right now if there had been no stimulus package and no financial bailout is receiving considerable attention. There's no way to know for sure, but I believe the economy would have been much worse off without these two policy interventions."

I also agree with President Obama that we have to trim programs where we can as a matter of *efficiency,* a word not often mentioned in the same sentence as *government.* When it comes to social safety net programs, we must have a renewed, transparent effort to root out abuse and corruption. It's not so much that all conservatives aren't willing to lend a hand to those truly in need, it's that they pessimistically believe there are too many freeloaders. I agree. There probably are, but you don't want to throw the baby out with the bathwater. What's important is that we reassure the American taxpayer that our government is working hard to expose the cheaters in our social programs. And to do that, let's use the same attitudes and standards when we examine corporate welfare.

As for those Wall Street leeches we bailed out? Damn right we have a right to oversee executive pay. Stephen Lerner, of the Service Employees International Union, was quoted in *Newsweek* after Goldman Sachs announced record bonuses less than a year after being bailed out by tax-payer dollars: "It's a combination of absurd and obscene that the same guys who crashed the economy . . . are now giving themselves even big-ger bonuses." In June 2009, Obama appointed an executive pay czar, Kenneth Feinberg, and gave him the authority to set the pay scale for executives at any company receiving government money. Some moaned about the constitutionality of the Feinberg appointment. But I think it is a reasonable strategy. Should we regulate the pay in other businesses? Of course not. What Obama is doing is simply providing oversight of a tax-payer investment, and the American people are behind him.

This is nowhere near as radical (or socialistic) as what Nixon did when he *twice* implemented national price and wage freezes in an at-tempt to address inflation. Nixon's strategy failed miserably, and Jimmy Carter and Fed chairman Paul Volcker were forced to address the prob-lem with high interest rates—which cost Carter the election against Ron-ald Reagan. It could be déjà vu all over again. A Democrat has been left to clean up the Republican mess and take the blame from a voting public with a ridiculously short memory.

UNFAIR TRADE DEALS UNDERMINED AMERICA

So greedy banks leave our economy unsound. And bad trade deals do, too. Back when the world was a bigger place, before lopsided trade agreements began flooding our shelves with foreign-made goods, unions helped organize workers, leading to fair wages and better working con-ditions. America bloomed.

Now we are witness to wilting American cities. The steady attack from overseas weakened, then destroyed, industry after industry. As con-sumers, we have benefited, but in many ways we have sold our soul to Walmart.

As it expands its dominance as the world's largest retailer, Walmart continues to squeeze every penny of profit out of each sale, forcing manufacturers to move factories to countries with cheap labor (and few labor or environmental standards) or die. Any U.S. factory hoping to compete must keep wages as low as possible. Meanwhile at home, to keep the competitive edge, Walmart seems to pay the lowest wages possible.

As long as you have a good job and can buy cheap goods, it's great. But, industry by industry, sector by sector, we are losing good jobs to China and India and Mexico in a race to the bottom line. When your number is up, things aren't so rosy, other than the color of the pink slip.

Many economists were shocked to see unemployment approach double digits in the summer of 2009, but I wasn't. For years, as I listened to my callers and traveled from city to city, I could see this coming. Good grief, unemployment in Detroit was pushing 30 percent in 2009, even as China officially became the world's largest auto market. What are the chances China will allow Detroit the same access to its marketplace that we allowed foreign car manufacturers in America?

One thing we have to do is to massage unfair trade agreements so that they become "more fair." I've long exhausted hopes of *exact* fairness. I'm fine with cutting some Third World countries a little slack in trade deals to help lift them up, but we don't need to grant favors to countries like China, countries that have feasted on whole American industries. It's like Nadal and Federer at Wimbledon—Federer doesn't need to spot Nadal any points at this stage of the game.

In reworking these trade agreements with China, India, Mexico, Japan, South Korea, and others, we have to make changes in ways that don't shock their economies too hard. But we do need to recognize that those economies have matured and should be able to compete straight-up sooner rather than later.

It is unlikely, in my view, anyway, that the U.S. economy will be as dynamic as China's or India's in the coming years. Here's why: As our economy boomed in the last century, the nation quite rightfully began to take on some legacy costs. We have slowly made progress with social programs to make sure that the very lowest on the economic ladder have some safety net. But we have not administrated wisely. As a nation we have not had the stomach to run these programs leaner or to fund them properly. Medicare, Medicaid, Social Security—these are good things, but with the baby boomers retiring, there is not nearly enough in the bank to fund those programs. And in addition, we need to move forward with health care reform. These are moral obligations—the things that must be done even though they are hard.

Economies tend to mature and level out with modest, predictable growth until the next technical innovation creates another spurt. Our rate of consumption when measured by our income as a nation is not sustainable. And we have to ask ourselves, Is the growth rate of our population—largely through immigration—sustainable?

As a nation we have to get these variables under control as best we can. I believe our economy will be less volatile in the future and might come to resemble those in Europe, with steady—not dramatic, but predictable— growth.

Meanwhile, we'll see China and India, and perhaps some other surprise players, make strong economic runs in the years ahead. There is great potential in South America, especially Brazil. If these nations are wise, they will apply some of their increasing largess to creating the social safety nets for their citizens that will decrease the distance between the top and bottom rungs of the economic ladder and lead to social order, which will lead to stability and peace.

THE IMPORTANCE OF UNIONS

On the home front, we need reenergized unions. I know, there are plenty of past negatives to overcome, but the principle is sound. If laborers are going to be treated like a commodity, they need to be organized. But I'd like to see a model in which union workers have real ownership and the prospect of substantial fiscal reward in years when the company is successful. A mistake some union negotiators made in the past was that while they were able to negotiate favorable contracts for the union workers, they burdened corporations with unsustainable legacy costs. However, with "skin in the game," unions would be much more willing to work for the success of the company and not just the success of the next labor agreement. It's the basic rule of capitalism. *Incentive.*

With outsourcing, the legs have been cut from underneath labor unions. Corporations just walked away from the negotiating table and took their companies with them—to China. We see what that has done to the country and to the workingman. Nobody wins. Wages have stagnated for the common working man and woman, while the rich are getting richer and richer.

From 2000 to 2007, according to the U.S. Census, median household income fell 0.6 percent and poverty inched up to 12.5 percent, all during an otherwise robust economy. In short, the average worker was seeing a steadily decreasing slice of the pie, even before the Great Recession.

The American worker will not regain any sort of upward economic traction without organizing, without a fight. Post-Reagan and post–Bushes I and II, the anti-worker voices in our country are still loud and getting louder. In December 2009, Fox News anchor Juliet Huddy argued on the air that to solve unemployment the American worker just had to work cheaper. She wasn't talking about Wall Street executives. "One school of thought says lowering the minimum wage will actually create more jobs," she said.

That's the ticket! What America needs is for the working poor to sacrifice just a little bit more—for their own good, of course. Minimum wage, by the way is $7.25 an hour, $15,000 a year. The poverty line is about $21,000 for a family of four.

That's the conservative plan in a nutshell. If you want a job, you just have to work cheaper. Yeah! Now we can all work for Walmart. Put Grandma's wheelchair up front. She can be a greeter. Increasingly, that is the thinking. The strength of unions has diminished through government complicity, because the government facilitated outsourcing, which is really union busting by another name; the American worker doesn't have much protection these days.

Meanwhile, low wages and lack of disposable income have hurt the entire marketplace. The irony of this anti-worker business model is that as corporations outsource, they are unwittingly practicing economic cannibalism by devouring the very workers they need to be consumers.

For our economy to work, labor and corporations have to become partners instead of adversaries. Look, I understand that there will always be an adversarial undercurrent to the relationship, but lots of people keep dogs and cats under the same roof. It works out. The ownership agreement worked out between the United Auto Workers and GM (17 percent) and Chrysler (55 percent) will be a good test. One thing is sure—it's pretty tough to go on strike against yourself.

The Employee Free Choice Act would make it easier for workers to form unions, and the Act stands to strengthen the bargaining power of all workers—which is why big business is so set against it. As a senator, Barack Obama was one of many bipartisan cosponsors of the Senate version (S. 842) of the bill, sponsored by the late Senator Edward Kennedy (D-MA) and Senator Arlen Specter (D-PA).

The house version (H.R. 1696) was sponsored in 2005 by Representative George Miller (D-CA), chairman of the House Committee on Education and Labor, who said during the bill's introduction, "The current process for forming unions is badly broken and so skewed in favor of those who oppose unions that workers must literally risk their jobs in order to form a union. Although it is illegal, one quarter of employers facing an organizing drive have been found to fire at least one worker who supports a union. The employer has all the power; the employer controls the information workers can receive, can force workers to attend anti-union meetings during work hours, can force workers to meet with supervisors who deliver anti-union messages, and can even imply that the business will close if the union wins."

Where would we be without unions? Unions and union organizers fought and died for child labor laws, the eight-hour workday, and safer working conditions. Unions pressured companies to pay women equal wages and defended workers against age discrimination. Through the years, many organizers were murdered for their efforts. At their core, unions defend not only workers' rights but *human rights*.

As of December 2009, the Employee Free Choice Act had not yet been brought to a vote, but the passage of this bill will be an important milestone along the road to empowering workers and rebuilding the middle class. America's economy will never be robust without a thriving middle class, and the success of unions will have much to say about that.

PAYING YOUR FAIR SHARE

Any time you have a fiscal policy that causes the richest 1 percent of American households to own more wealth than the bottom 90 percent, you've got a problem. The last time America had such a drastic difference between the haves and the have-nots was before the Great Depression. This more recent handout to the wealthy picked up warp speed with tax cuts for fat cats under Ronald Reagan, who lowered the top tax rate from 70 to 28 percent (it was 35 percent in 2009), and culminated with tax cuts for the rich under Bush II in the midst of two wars—something unprecedented in American history. (Taxes have increased in every previous U.S. war, except when they stayed level during the war against Mexico in the 1840s.)

Where was the sacrifice for the wars in Iraq and Afghanistan? Bush and Cheney fought these wars with credit cards, and now that they are out of office, the statement has come in the mail.

Meanwhile, überconservatives, having slept through straight talk about fiscal matters for eight years, are *now* hypocritically concerned about the national debt. These Rip Van Republicans want to use the Bush-Cheney national debt to squelch everything from health care to stimulus programs, seemingly clueless that the way to kick-start the economy is to get more disposable income back in the hands of consumers.

Any student of Business 101 understands that when expenditures exceed income, it's a good idea to increase income. In this case, we need to tighten our belts and do what Bush I and Bill Clinton did, and that is to raise taxes on the top bracket. Bush I went from 28 to 31 percent and Clinton, during the largest economic boom ever in America, made it 39.6 percent. The nation thrived! Clinton was balancing the budget! He also tightened up welfare.

When it comes to Social Security and Medicare, I believe in means testing. I know, I know, we all paid in, but does Bill Gates really need Social Security? If you have the means to do without the programs, you should. We all contribute to aspects of the infrastructure that we may not use but that are there for the greater good. Childless couples pay property taxes, and most of that goes to education. We have to consider the greater good if we are to be a greater country.

I see the logic of a progressive tax. But I sure as heck don't support a punitive tax code. I don't think Americans making $250,000 are necessarily rich, but most of us can afford to pay a little more per earned dollar than those making $21,000 a year, and if paying a little more is what it takes to keep the country safe and strong, sign me up.

Republicans have successfully made the word "taxes" a dirty word for thirty years, but taxes are a necessity. It's a matter of paying your dues as a member of this club we call America. You bet we ought to look for efficiencies where we can, and we ought to fight tooth and nail against increasing taxes, but in the end, we must accept that a certain level of taxation is the price of being an American.

The estate tax is a good idea. It keeps the playing field level. What's wrong with the Gateses and Buffetts and the Oprahs and the Waltons (and I don't mean John-Boy) giving back to the country that gave them the opportunities to succeed? What's healthy about a pubescent billionaire who was born into it? Hey, I want my kids to have a little something when I'm gone, but not an empire. Working, not inheriting, builds character.

My father was a member of the Greatest Generation. I am ashamed to be a member of the Greediest Generation, and selfishness has been my generation's legacy to this point. Bush and Cheney left us with one hell of a mess and one hell of a bill. Do we have the moral character to clean up the mess and pay the bill, or are we going to pass it on to our children? It's not too late to redeem ourselves.

Pillar #3: Feed the Country

I live in two worlds. One is on the streets of Manhattan. The other is the lake and farm country on the Minnesota–North Dakota border. I see both of these worlds up close and personal, and I wish everyone could, because if there is a disconnect in America, it is between these worlds.

I can barely begin to express the frustration I have when I hear the East Coast intelligentsia editorialize in such an uninformed manner against farm subsidies. I want to grab them by the collar and say, "Do you realize it is *your* grocery bill that is being subsidized?"

Don't any of them know what it is like to have a little cowshit on your boots, live in a small town, or have a cup of coffee with a rancher? I have a small home in Mott, out in western North Dakota, where I go to hunt pheasants. Living in Mott part-time also keeps me in touch with the farming and ranching communities, and let me tell you, these good folks bear no relation to the people castigated on the editorial pages of the eastern press.

THE FARM BILL ALLOWS YOU TO EAT CHEAP!

We have a cheap food philosophy in this country that was born out of the Great Depression and a society whose European immigrants remembered all too well the great famines of Europe. According to U.S. Department of Agriculture statistics, in 1929, 23 percent of family income went to food. In 2008, that percentage was 9.6.

And people want to complain about a safety net for the people who have helped deliver this economic miracle. The farm folks I know aren't getting rich. If they were, you'd be paying a hell of a lot more than 9.6 percent.

The cost of subsidies to you? *A fraction of a percent* of the federal budget. Did you know food stamps, school lunch, and other nutrition programs account for *50 percent* of current Farm Bill spending—about $44 billion per year—about what it costs for four months of war in Iraq. While major industry has repressed wages, as poverty has inched upward, the Farm Bill is picking up the slack by feeding poor Americans! The Farm Bill is a poverty buster, though that's not something you'll hear from editorial writers in the major newspapers. They focus on the aspects of the Farm Bill that subsidize those who don't need the help, but in doing so they miss the big picture. Unfortunately, there are always people who will find a way to "game" a program. So no, this program is not perfect, and guys from farm states know it. They know the program is too heavily weighted in favor of Big Ag instead of the traditional family farm.

Senator Byron Dorgan (D-ND) and Senator Charles E. Grassley (R-IA) have unsuccessfully tried to cap federal payments for farming couples at $250,000 annually. The way the system works now, with slim profit margins, it encourages mega farms. The days when a farmer could make a good living on a few hundred acres are gone. Even "family" farms commonly extend over thousands of tillable acres. One of the downsides of the current system is a shrinking of rural communities and a waning of the work ethic and family values that spring from such communities. Still, for now, fewer farmers producing more bushels does mean lower grocery bills for us all.

THE MERITS OF SMALL FARMS VS. BIG AG

When it comes to the safety and security of our food supply, we are much more secure with a vast network of small, independent producers than we are trusting big corporations. There's an old adage: "Don't put all your eggs in one basket," and there's wisdom in that statement.

Late in 2008, the nation's largest poultry producer declared bankruptcy. Pilgrim's Pride Corporation, with 25 percent of the market share, filed Chapter 11 because of high overhead, weak market conditions, and a heavy debt load. Pilgrim's Pride supplies Kentucky Fried Chicken, operates thirty-five chicken processing plants and eleven prepared-food plants. Although the company continues to operate, its bankruptcy casts a shadow on the security of our food supply. Two companies—Tyson and Pilgrim's Pride—produce about half of the chickens in America today. To borrow a phrase from the financial crisis, they have become too big to fail.

In the crowded Big Ag conditions that produce a chicken for slaughter in four to six weeks, disease could wipe out millions of birds pretty quick. Birds are genetically engineered just as crops are for disease resistance and quick growth, but what happens if a disease mutates and kills them all? There's something to be said for the diversity that family farms have traditionally ensured.

We all realize that there are efficiencies in large corporations, but when it comes to something as personal and important as the food we put into our bodies, we ought to expend every effort to maintain a healthy supply, and that means supporting the independent producer. People seem to be gravitating in that direction. We see more farmers' markets springing up. More and more, city dwellers look for ways to buy meat on the hoof. There's a certain comfort that comes from knowing how an animal was raised and processed.

The turkeys I see in the wild in western North Dakota bear little resemblance to the birds sold in stores, which have such large breasts they are actually too fat to breed by conventional means and are propagated through artificial insemination. However, "heritage" breeds are making a comeback. These varieties are typically tastier and bear a closer resemblance to wild turkeys.

As a sportsman, I can tell you that a wild goose, duck, pheasant, grouse, partridge, or turkey makes a far better meal than anything I can find from a factory farm.

PROFIT TRUMPS FOOD SAFETY

As the poultry industry has consolidated, the incidence of food-borne illnesses has increased. A North Carolina State University study found that eight of every ten poultry carcasses in North Carolina were positive for campylobacter, one of the most frequent sources of food-borne illness in people and a leading cause of death from such illness.

According to the World Health Organization, "in industrialized countries, the percentage of the population suffering from food-borne diseases each year has been reported to be up to 30 percent. In the United States of America (USA), for example, around *76 million cases* of food-borne diseases, resulting in 325,000 hospitalizations and 5,000 deaths, are estimated to occur each year" (emphasis mine).

That's astonishing. The American dinner table has become more dangerous than a war zone. This is happening in *industrialized* countries! Plain and simple, it's because profit has begun to trump food safety and consumer protection. Take for instance COOL, the country of origin labeling legislation, which was passed in 2002. COOL would label foods so consumers could decide if they wanted an American steak or one from Canada, where there have been well-publicized incidents of

mad cow disease. But bureaucratic and legislative stall tactics have delayed the implementation of these rules. Why? Big conglomerates think
it would hurt their business if you knew where your food originated.

Without COOL, American food conglomerates can buy cheap food
overseas, which leverages down the price American producers can get
for their produce. But knowing that food safety oversight is even more
lacking in some countries other than in our own, shouldn't we, as consumers, be accorded the basic respect of knowing where the food on our
plates came from?

Do I think mad cow is a serious issue in Canada? No. But I ought to
be able to decide if I want to buy American, Mexican, or Australian beef.
Good grief, I know my boxer shorts come from China, but don't have a
clue about my T-bone!

The monopolization of the food industry by just a few corporations
is chilling. It drives small producers out of business and puts the control
of our food supply in the hands of just a few. In 2005, Smithfield, Tyson,
Swift & Company, and Cargill owned nearly 64 percent of the hog
market. Also, according to 2005 statistics, Tyson, Cargill, Swift & Company, and National Beef Packing slaughtered 84 percent of the cattle in
the United States.

It's not a stretch to suggest that that kind of market share creates an
opportunity to manipulate prices. A cattlemen's watchdog group, R-CALF,
sued Tyson, but after a federal jury ruled for the cattlemen, the 8th Cir-
cuit Court of Appeals overturned the verdict. In June 2009, Tyson, in
what R-CALF says was an effort to intimidate, sought attorneys' fees from
Herman Schumacher, a Herreid, South Dakota, cattleman, who led the
lawsuit against Tyson. Schumacher, who refused to pay, returned home
one day to find U.S. marshals seizing his property.

Schumacher says the official edict taped on his door by the marshals
was a warning to any other rancher with the notion to stand up against
violations of the 1921 Packers and Stockyards Act, which prohibits packers from engaging in "unfair and deceptive practices, manipulating

prices, creating a monopoly or conspiring to aid in unlawful acts." In our justice system, deep pockets win out. The rich and the big corporations use the courts to financially bully enemies into submission.

Of the Four Pillars, Feeding the Country is the most important one. Nothing else happens unless the people are fed. Americans have become accustomed to low prices and overall high safety standards, but consolidation and market manipulation have eroded both. The U.S. Department of Agriculture has seemingly looked the other way—in part because urban Americans don't grasp what is at stake. But I have no doubt that unless we challenge these food monopolies now, we will regret it later.

While it is easy to eat cheap in America, it isn't cheap to eat *healthy*. I've heard some commentators cite obesity rates as evidence that Americans are doing well. It's quite the opposite. Inexpensive prepackaged, starchy, corn syrup–laden products fill our supermarket shelves, and that has led to increases in obesity, diabetes, and other life-threatening ailments. Healthy fruits, vegetables, meats, and whole grain breads cost more than many people can afford. According to a study by Adam Drewnowski of the University of Washington, a healthy two-thousand-calorie diet could cost *almost 10 times as much* as one comprised of junk food. Meanwhile, it takes more junk food to feel satisfied, so people quite predictably overeat. A Scripps Research Institute study concludes that the brain responds to junk food just as it does to heroin.

Little Debbie is dealing smack? And she seemed like such a nice girl.

I don't see any way that we can completely solve our health care crisis without improving the way we eat, an improvement that could take generations of education. And we need to make sure we have food security. A diverse network of small producers is essential, and we ought to support the legislation that will help make that possible. As long as other countries subsidize their farmers, it is only fair that we afford ours a level playing field.

We have seen what unfair trade does to America. Unfair trade began as a shift of our manufacturing base to other countries. If we allow our market to become flooded with cheaper food from other countries, as we do other goods, this may seem great for the consumer in the short haul, but it will drive farmers off the land and destabilize our ability to feed the nation. We must never allow ourselves to be dependent on imports to feed our citizens.

In a perfect world, American farmers could compete handily, with no trade barriers, but Europe is in no hurry to give up subsidies for their farmers. Expect subsidies to continue but to be slowly reduced globally.

In the meantime, it is in our best interest to find new trading partners. Cuba, a country I broadcast from during an agricultural trade mission, is an obvious candidate. Healthy trade won't necessarily damage relationships internationally; it could actually go a long way toward settling tensions in some corners of the world.

Pillar #4: Educate the People

Later in this book I will make the case that health care should be a basic right for every American. I feel the same way about education. I don't believe economic circumstances should dictate whether any American has the opportunity to go to college.

As the son of a teacher and as a student who was bused to the slums of Norfolk, Virginia, for high school, I have seen different aspects of the educational spectrum. In many classrooms, students are thriving, but in others, we are failing them miserably. When we fail to educate all of our children, our society begins to fail. Education in America is a crisis that really is not talked about enough.

When we fail to keep students in school, they end up on the streets and become part of what Marian Wright Edelman, one of the leading children's advocates in the world, calls the "cradle to prison syndrome." Her website, childrensdefense.org, states, "Nationally, 1 in 3 Black and 1 in 6 Latino boys born in 2001 are at risk of imprisonment during their lifetime. . . . States spend about three times as much money per prisoner as per public school pupil."

The fact is, and I've seen it, poor kids don't get the same breaks other kids do.

Poverty becomes a cycle of hopelessness from one generation to the next, and as a country we ought to be grappling with the fact that the richest country on earth has one of the highest poverty levels of any industrialized nation. According to a government report, *America's Children: Key National Indicators of Well-Being,* nearly one in five American children was living in poverty in 2007.

There's no silver bullet solution to such pervasive poverty and lack of opportunity, but part of the solution is addressing the disintegration of the American family and the poverty that is closely related to single-parent households.

Let's connect the dots. Birth certificate records show 40 percent of the babies born in America in 2007 were born to single mothers. Meanwhile, the National Commission on Children reports that three out of four children from single-parent families will experience poverty before they turn eleven, and the Department of Health and Human Services says that fatherless children are twice as likely to drop out of school. No government program is going to solve this—however, better employment opportunities can. And as a society we need to have a national discussion about the importance of families. The concept of family isn't an anachronism, it is a cornerstone of society. I know some people will naturally bristle because this has been a right wing bullet point for so long, but it's time for us to take back the issue. Those right wingers like to talk a good game. Let's *play* a good game by at least creating a social and educational framework that allows people from all social strata to succeed.

Now let's look at schools themselves.

It's no secret that primary education in America lags in comparison with many other industrialized countries. In eighth-grade math skills, according to a 2007 *USA Today* report, our best performing state, Massachusetts, with 51 percent of the students proficient, was well behind Singapore (73 percent), Hong Kong (68 percent), Korea (65 percent), Taiwan (61 percent), and Japan (57 percent). When given the choice, most high school students opt out of Advanced Math, Physics, and Science, says the National Science Foundation. That lack of enthusiasm suggests that there is something terribly wrong with the way we are teaching our kids.

In some cases, it is the teachers. Every school has a teacher who cannot teach but who keeps hanging on because no one has the guts to deal with the issue. By and large, I support teachers unions, but let's get real. Not every teacher is competent or worth defending. The stakes are too high to allow inept teachers to retain their positions. For children, these years from elementary school through high school are their only chance to learn to read and write. For every bad teacher allowed to remain in place, hundreds of children lose the opportunity of a lifetime. You, as a member of a school board or as an involved patron of the school district, can play a huge role in supporting great teachers and not renewing poor ones. When it comes to education, grassroots efforts can make a dramatic difference.

THE TEXTBOOK DUMB DOWN

A 2006 MSNBC.com report by correspondent Alex Johnson touches on an issue most people don't know about or consider—the sorry state of textbooks. More than ever, just as agenda-driven networks too often tell their viewers what they want to hear, so do textbook publishers, who must appeal to school boards filled with religious zealots on one extreme and granola-munching atheists on the other. When you consider that Texas and California control one third of the textbook market purchases, you can begin to imagine how these textbooks are being crafted to sell to school boards.

The textbook industry has consolidated to the point that there are now just the Big Four—Pearson, McGraw-Hill, Reed Elsevier, and Houghton Mifflin. Consolidation to that extent is never good, because when you don't have to compete, *you don't have to get better.* Profit then matters more than performance. When capitalism allows monopolies to form unchecked, you get the same kind of stagnation you find with unchecked socialism. Ironic.

Diane Ravitch, a senior official in the Department of Education who served Presidents George H. W. Bush and Bill Clinton, said, "[Textbooks] are sanitized to avoid offending anyone who might complain at textbook adoption hearings in big states, they are poorly written, they are burdened with irrelevant and unedifying content, and they reach for the lowest common denominator."

Monopolies are changing the way we live and *think.* What's the solution in education?

POLITICS IN THE CLASSROOM

It seems to me that our schools have become an ideological battleground, places in which being politically correct is more important than being correct. I am a student of history, but most of the real history I have learned has come through my own research. No one taught me in high school that the CIA under Eisenhower helped overthrow the government in Iran in 1953. When you know that, you begin to understand why the Iranian people overthrew the shah. Instead, when American hostages were taken, we had a huge story with no perspective. In a sense, textbooks have been cheerleaders for America, more concerned with the political correctness of the day than with objective facts.

Today, a conservative group of shrill Christian fundamentalists have become the new know-nothings. They don't want evolution taught in the schools despite millions of years of fossils and other scientific evidence, which they feel contradicts the Bible. Polar caps are melting around us, yet climate change doubters abound—and affect what children are learning in school. Information has become so political that we are endangering our futures by withholding crucial facts from students. (I just didn't understand how my belief in climate change could be liberal until Stephen Colbert famously quipped at a 2006 White House Correspondents Dinner, "Reality has a well-known liberal bias.")

I have a friend whose fifth-grade son's dim-witted teacher told the class the Iraq War was in retaliation for 9/11. When the boy correctly insisted that no Iraqis had been on the planes that crashed into the World Trade Center or the Pentagon, he was "corrected." So he went home, researched on the Internet, and handed the proof to the teacher the next day. Not surprisingly, the boy did not do well in her class. During student-teacher conferences, this first-year teacher told the boy's parents the key to their son's academic performance was church, a statement you can well imagine they took like a poke in the eye.

Must we really incorporate religion into science and succumb to political pressure to include creationism in the curriculum? My faith is strong enough that I don't feel threatened by an atheist point of view. I look in wonder at the sky at night, and I have to believe something greater than I created it.

Must we constantly fight parental efforts to ban certain books? Why do we fear that "thoughts" might somehow infect our children? That shows a complete lack of faith in one's parenting skills. The politicization of the classroom reached a ridiculous high when President Obama sought to address America's students in 2009. The political blowback from the right wingers was so intense that many schools chose not to allow students to hear Obama's remarks, to avoid controversy.

My friend Tony Bender, an author and columnist, wrote, "The Republicans screamed that it was some kind of indoctrination. Turns out, it was. Obama subversively encouraged them to stay in school and graduate! Well, you know what education does to people, don't you? Turns them into Democrats!"

COLLEGE MAKES CENTS

According to 2006 U.S. Census statistics, college graduates make about *$23,000 more a year* than high school graduates. Those with advanced degrees make about $80,000, while high school dropouts average less than $20,000. Show those numbers to your kid the next time your kid's report card comes out. Because income and education are so closely tied together, it stands to reason that those with the financial wherewithal in the first place hold the advantage. Not only can they afford college, but they can afford the best colleges. A student from a working family of less means may not be able to afford college at all, and you can see how that negative cycle is perpetuated—an undereducated head of household earns less, making it less likely that person's children can afford college.

The right thing to do is to make education a civil right just like health care. Some European countries subsidize college student living expenses, and I think that should be our long-term goal. It's worth considering especially for our veterans, who deserve every break we can give them. But we know that won't happen overnight. President Obama is on the right track with his proposed annual $4,000 tax credit for students in exchange for community service, but it is a small first step.

As you consider the best education for your children, know that not everyone in this new economy will be wearing suits and ties. There is tremendous opportunity in the trades—plumbing, electrical, construction—because these are good-paying jobs that can't be shipped overseas. A two-year community college education could open the doors to many things—perhaps even your child's own business.

THE STUDENT LOAN TRAP

Man, it kills me to see so many college graduates looking for a job while huge student loan payments hang over their heads like dark clouds. Too many people fall into the student loan trap. Don't get me wrong. I'm not against student loans, but anytime you borrow, you need to have your eyes wide open. Watch for sharks!

It is imperative that we make higher education if not free, then affordable—and that we clean up the seamy world of student loans. Through the Federal Family Education Loan Program, lenders have been collecting generous subsidies for making virtually risk-free loans. This sort of thing never ceases to astonish me. The very financial sectors that preach the virtues of risk-based capitalism want a sure thing from the government.

The Student Aid and Fiscal Responsibility Act of 2009 could change all that by getting rid of the unscrupulous middlemen and saving taxpayers $87 billion over a decade. The savings would fund a $40 billion increase in Pell Grants, $10 billion in community college upgrades, and $8 billion for early childhood education.

Many colleges, though, are against this act. Why? The dirty little secret is that some of them are in cahoots with the lenders. In exchange for giving a lender "preferred status," even if that lender did not offer the best packages, some collage bureaucrats received kickbacks for listing a lender's student loan offerings as "preferred." According to the *Washington Post,* a financial aid director at Johns Hopkins University "accepted more than $130,000 from eight lending industry companies during her tenure, twice as much money as previously disclosed."

When you consider all of the evidence—when you do the math—why wouldn't we want to pass the bill? The argument from Republicans (surprise) is that the bill would cause five thousand layoffs in the private lending sector. Are you kidding me? This is like taking bank robbers off the street—not bankers. Good grief, the financial industry damn near buried the economy; they have screwed middle-class Americans every way you can get screwed. *You* bailed them out—WE bailed them out with OUR tax dollars—and now we should allow this crooked little game to continue? We need to get our priorities straight. We need to stick up for the students.

The State of the Four Pillars

There you have it—the Four Pillars: Defend the Nation, Establish a Sound Fiscal Policy, Feed the Country, and Educate the People. It's pretty basic. If we do these four things well, we will thrive. If one pillar crumbles, the rest begin to wobble.

So, how would Professor Schultz grade the state of the pillars today?

Defend the Nation—C+

Certainly our intelligence network is better now than it was a decade ago. President Obama's outreach to other countries has put us on the path to build more coalitions and isolate terrorists and rogue states, and his efforts toward nuclear disarmament have made us safer. His is an enlightened approach—he recognizes that an insular, isolationist approach and a go-it-alone attitude is destined to fail.

Our soldiers have been valiant, but the Bush administration left our forces overcommitted and undermanned. Our inability to extricate ourselves from Afghanistan and Iraq means less flexibility for our military assets. Despite Dick Cheney's assertions that the Bush administration made us safer, countries like Iran, North Korea, Russia, and China, understanding our vulnerabilities, were emboldened during the Bush administration. It's going to take some time to rebuild our military and reassure the world of our strength.

Internally, we need to examine our role as an arms dealer to the world. And we need to do some serious soul-searching about the potentially intrusive role of technology in our defense plans; if we can't uphold the Constitution while defending our country, what exactly are we defending?

Establish a Sound Fiscal Policy—D+

And that's an improvement from the F the Obama administration inherited from the Bush administration. TARP and the stimulus package saved this country and world from the much more serious meltdown that could have happened. However, the financial sector of this country still remains predatory in nature, and Congress has not gone far enough to rein it in. The energy and health care industries continue to slowly bleed the life out of the economy. Until those issues and our trade imbalances are brought into check, the country will be on shaky financial footing. I believe the president and some members of Congress are committed to debt reduction. The test is whether the American people are willing to make the necessary sacrifices.

Feed the Country—B–

The cost of food in America is remarkably low, and food is abundant. The bad news is, much of it is overprocessed and just plain bad for you. Monopolies also threaten the supply and quality of our food. Here's a case of the frog in the pot set to boil. We may feel comfortable for now, but eventually the water will boil and it will be a crisis too late for us to avoid. We need to look ahead. It's imperative that we do all we can to support diversity—small farmers—any way we can, while diminishing the strength of food monopolies.

Educate the People—C–

We can do so much better. We talk about a Manhattan Project for this and that, so why not one for education? Our true enduring greatness as a nation rests on our ability to educate a creative, enlightened population. Until every citizen has an equal opportunity to be educated, we will not have succeeded. Education, like health care, should not be "for profit" but available for all as a right of citizenship. The more educated Americans are, the greater we can become.

CHAPTER THREE

HEALTH CARE

Your Inalienable Right

EXHAUSTED . . . I WAS DEAD TIRED WHEN I MADE A GUEST APPEAR-
ance on MSNBC's *Morning Joe* show on December 17, 2009. Just a few days
before that I had been broadcasting from Kansas City at a free health clinic,
seeing something I never thought I would see in America—thousands of
good people, most of them the working poor, some of them the struggling
middle class, all lined up for health care they could not otherwise afford.
The clinics were Keith Olbermann's idea, and donations from some
twenty-five thousand MSNBC viewers made them possible. I spent two
days broadcasting from Kansas City. It was emotionally wrenching.

Strung out from traveling, tired, battling one helluva cold, and just
plain heartbroken about what I had seen, I told Joe Scarborough's viewers that morning what I thought about the compromised health care bill
on the table that day. Although it improved many things, it contained no
public option and, as I saw it, provided no real competition for the insurance companies. "The president never drew a line in the sand . . . he
hasn't been tough," I said. "Barack Obama is not listening to his base."

Well, *somebody* was listening to me, because moments later, a remarkable thing happened. One of the president's closest advisors, David

Axelrod, called the show, and we got into it. "Where's the competition?" I asked. "People in this country right now—the progressives—don't believe that the White House has stood up to the insurance industry."

Axelrod responded, "Ed, let me ask you a question. Why is the insurance industry so vigorously opposing this bill? . . . We fought for years as progressives for a patient's bill of rights. Everything that was in that patient's bill of rights is now enshrined in this legislation. And yet people say, let's just throw it away [the health care bill], we don't need it anymore. Why is the insurance industry fighting us so hard?"

"Respectfully, Mr. Axelrod, I'll answer your question if you answer mine," I said. "I'll answer your question: [The insurance industry has] the money to play a shell game on the American people. They're creating this facade that [the health care plan you propose] is really bad for them. It's not, it's a handout."

It is, too. The insurance companies were crying wolf over the Senate health care plan, doing some serious melodrama, and then laughing all the way to the bank. Wall Street sure thought so. Insurance stocks went through the roof! C'mon! Don't piss on my leg and tell me it's raining.

The proposed legislation mandated that all Americans must buy insurance from a private company. Yes, those who can't afford it would get government subsidies, but the bottom line was: The insurance companies would get 31 million new customers and no pesky government insurance option to compete against them. I call that a handout.

My exchange with Axelrod reflected two things. First of all, it reflected the angst Americans were feeling about all this. Second, on a personal level, it reflected the chill that had developed between the White House and me during the course of the health care debate.

I carried plenty of water for Barack Obama during the campaign, because I thought he was the right man at the right time, and I still think that. But the White House has developed rabbit ears. They don't understand that I may be one of the best friends they have, because I am not an enabler. I tell it like it is—at least how I see it—and a lesson I learned long ago is that the best friend you can have is the guy who tells you what you don't want to hear but need to. You have to be able to differentiate the tough love from an attack.

One of the most infuriating things about writing this book has been that while I've been writing it, the fight for health care reform has been a real-time emotional roller-coaster ride. The public option is in! No, it's dead! It's alive! No, it's been traded for Medicare expansion! And on and on it went. When Scott Brown won the Senate seat Ted Kennedy had held for nearly fifty years, it cost the Democrats their filibuster-proof majority, and threatened to undo the bill.

Every day, I felt it was my duty to be fully informed on every twist and turn in the legislative process in Washington, so I could fight for health care each afternoon on the radio and each weekday evening on MSNBC. I had a pulpit during a crucial time for health justice in the United States, and I was determined to use it well. I'm a redhead who wears his heart on his sleeve, so all the twists and turns just about did me in sometimes. Some days I felt wrung out!

Why, I wondered, can't we come together as a country? Why can't we do the right thing, which I know it is in our nature to do? Why must we move forward in such excruciating increments?

None of us, including me, has learned patience. The twenty-four-hour news cycle drives our emotions. But it shouldn't. This is the age of instant gratification, and we *expect* our presidents to solve every problem in the first year. That's insane.

In light of the fractious nature of Congress, the obstructionist policies of conservatives, and the power of the health care industry, it is clear that the journey to where we need to go with health care will be one measured over decades.

In my mind there are a few things that ought to be basic human rights in our system. I believe every person has an equal right to a good education. I believe every American has the right to retire from the workplace in dignity, with a reasonable standard of living. And in my heart I know that it is morally bankrupt to base the quality of health care on the size of the recipient's wallet—to have some insurance company bean counter making a decision that should be left to a patient and the patient's doctor.

Reasonable access to health care is a basic civil right.

That said, the citizen has some responsibilities, too, and we'll get to that—*settle down, righties!* As a progressive in this politically correct world, don't you get tired of feeling like you have to placate archconservatives every few sentences to let them know that, like them, you believe in personal responsibility? Geez! Living under this suffocating Republican influence for so long has us all walking around with our sphincters so tight, if we started eating coal we could crap diamonds.

The fact of the matter is, there are far more things that unite us as Americans than divide us, and one of them is health care. A 2008 survey commissioned by the Commonwealth Fund reported that 82 percent of more than one thousand surveyed thought the system needed to be overhauled. *You think?* Other surveys showed a majority of Americans favored a government-run option to compete with private insurers. Meanwhile, the House Republican leader, Representative John Boehner of Ohio, claimed "I'm still trying to find the first American to talk to who is in favor of the public option." That's the equivalent of not being able to find your ass with both hands.

Pre-Obama, the United States spent *twice* per capita what other developed nations spend on health care. Still, life expectancy in America, at 78.11 years, ranks fiftieth in the world. Canada is eighth with a life expectancy of 81.3. Not a single major industrialized nation with national health care ranks lower than the United States.

Macau has the longest life expectancy in the world (84.36), and Japan, at number 3, is the highest ranked industrial nation (82.12).

Meanwhile, U.S. infant mortality is 6.26 per 1,000 births, forty-fifth best, ranking just behind Cuba. Singapore is at the top with a 2.31 infant mortality rate.

Tell me again that health care in the United States is the best in the world.

If you're wondering how Singapore does it, a nationalized health insurance plan there is funded by payroll deductions, some government subsidies, and through price controls. Many Singaporeans also have supplemental insurance for services not covered by the government. The country spends 3 percent of GDP on health care, compared to 17 percent ($2.4 trillion) in the United States. Compare that to 10.9 percent of the GDP spent on health care in Switzerland and 9.7 percent in Canada.

Someday we will come to the conclusion that universal health care is the optimum solution. We already have a program that works—Medicare—all we have to do is expand it to everyone. We will find it makes the most sense for our economy as a whole and, more importantly, that it is the moral thing to do. The frustrating thing about this cause is that we can only get the votes for baby steps. "You can't pass legislation with polls," Senator Kent Conrad told me on my radio show. "You need votes—and we don't have the votes." What? For the first time since 1979, the Democrats had sixty votes in the Senate, and still I was hearing "Well, you know, Eddie, we jest can't get 'er dun."

You're kidding, right? You're telling a guy who, like millions of others, busted his ass for a victory for Barack Obama and a Senate majority, all on the promise of change, that the Democrats are still kowtowing to the minority! "Excuse me there, would it be OK if we passed a little health care legislation?"

Those sixty votes lasted just a year, and the Democrats failed to take advantage of the opportunity.

What the hell! What would Bush have done with sixty votes? We'd be in Iran by now! The Dixie Chicks would be in jail and Toby Keith would be the secretary of defense. What is with the Democratic Party? I keep hearing about these Chicago Thug Politics. Yeah? Well, gimme some! The opportunities afforded by a sixty-vote Senate majority come

around as often as Haley's Comet or Dick Cheney telling the truth—
and the Democrats acted like they were on life support. Where's our
Tom DeLay? Why, as Democrats, can't we put the hammer down?

OK, OK! As we discovered, the sixty-vote majority was strictly theoretical, anyway. Smokey Joe Lieberman (I-CT) long ago abandoned
any fealty to the Democratic Caucus. (Note the use of the word "Democratic." I find the use by conservatives of the term "Democrat Party" in-
sulting. They can't stand our association with democratic principles,
apparently. We don't call them the Republic Party, do we?)

I appreciate the president's efforts to try to work with Republicans,
but they are too invested in his failure. Olive branches are not working,
so at least try a bigger branch, Mr. President! Sometimes you do need
a big stick. Barack Obama needs to set aside Lincoln for a while and
model LBJ. Heck, Landslide Lyndon was known to pick up senators by
the ears! That's how I heard it, anyway.

Republican opposition to health care reform has little to do with the
actual issue. It's about taking the president down, as Tim Dickinson ex-
plained in *Rolling Stone:* "Behind the scenes, top Republicans—including
House Minority Whip Eric Cantor, Minority Leader John Boehner and
the chairman of the GOP's Senate steering committee, Jim DeMint—
worked hand-in-glove with the organizers of the town brawls. Their
goal was not only to block health care reform but to bankrupt President
Obama's political capital before he could move on to other key items
on his agenda, including curbing climate change and expanding labor
rights. As DeMint told an August [2009] teleconference of nearly 20,000
town-hall activists, 'If we can stop him on this, the administration won't
be able to go on to cap and trade, card check and the other things they
want to do.'"

When I think of good Americans suffering through health and financial issues while politicians play games with their lives in Washington . . .
well, how can that not just infuriate you? They don't seem to care about
doing what's right. They just want the Democrats to lose!

Strategically, the White House made some mistakes, too.

First of all, Obama took the ultimate health care fix—universal coverage—off the table early. Well, any horse trader knows you don't give ground right out of the gate. You need to leave room to negotiate. So you start high and negotiate from there. Seemingly, Obama started at the point he thought was politically achievable, which did not give him room to move. From a political standpoint, your supporters feel sold out from the beginning and your detractors are angry because they don't feel you have given up enough in the process.

All of that may well have been a moot point because it seems the Republicans care more about winning than doing the right thing. And maybe sixty consistent votes in the Senate was a pipe dream. Democrats have never organized as tightly as the Republicans. You want sixty votes on any issue? You probably need seventy Democrats because many of the Democrats come from conservative districts. Really, in some respects in America, we have two conservative parties, one is just less extreme than the other.

Here's the landscape: We are expecting one hundred senators with job security, a great pension, and the best health care on the planet to fix this problem. The institutions in the health care industry that don't want change are filling the campaign war chests of their favorite lawmakers. Health industry lobbyists outnumber lawmakers in Washington by at least four to one.

For all the mistakes and foot dragging on the part of Democrats, do you want to know the biggest reason why you and your children will not be seeing universal health care anytime soon? Not only did the Republicans oppose reform in a strategic effort to damage Obama, they set the table for this bitter feast by helping George W. Bush blow up the budget. Had Bush been fiscally responsible, the debt would have been erased and the nation could have much more easily afforded an investment in universal health care.

YOUR CHOICE: FINANCIAL RUIN OR DYING

If you don't have health insurance and you come down with a big medical problem, you must choose one of two options—financial ruin or dying. And in *my America,* we have to debate the politics of it all? Let me tell you, brother, when you are circling the drain, you just want a lifeline. Just a chance at making it. Just a few more heartbeats to spend some time with the grandkids, to see a few more sunrises. That's what this is all about.

When it has been tried, socialized medicine has worked. Take Medicare for instance. Could you find ten retired Republicans in America willing to give up their Medicare benefits? Of course not. Not even the dozens of congressmen on Medicare would give it up. So what's the big argument about? This one was decided long ago. Opponents are wrong now and they were wrong in 1964 when LBJ delivered on Medicare.

In 1964 the Saint of Conservatism, Ronald Reagan, blasted Medicare in a speech. "Will you resist the temptation to get a government handout for your community? Realize that the doctor's fight against socialized medicine is your fight. We can't socialize the doctors without socializing the patients. Recognize that government invasion of public power is eventually an assault upon your own business."

Let's break that down.

Handouts for Whom

Who's really getting the handouts in our health care system? In 2003, President George W. Bush drastically expanded the Medicare program with Medicare Part D (which subsidizes prescription drug costs for Medicare recipients), which I guess was OK, although it was as much a benefit to elderly Americans as a license to commit highway robbery for the pharmaceutical companies, which get to sell drugs under the program without any pesky negotiations to drive down prices. Oh, *that* was fiscally responsible.

Socializing Patients

I guess Medicare makes Grandma and Grandpa Commies. I'll bet if you check the closet, you'll find a statue of Karl Marx. Well, you had better hope Grandma and Grandpa have plenty in the bank, because according to Fidelity Investments, retiring elderly couples will need $250,000–$300,000 in savings to afford most basic medical coverage.

An Assault on Business

Are you kidding me? The assault on businesses has been the inability to be competitive while shouldering employee health care costs. From a competitive standpoint in the global economy, doesn't it seem ludicrous to expect our businesses to start in such a deep hole? The natural reaction is for businesses to relocate, taking away American jobs, in the interest of competitiveness. Yes, there are all sorts of other factors, from tax havens to the disparity in environmental regulations, but, ironically, the burden of health care has become unsustainable for the free market to bear.

According to Micah Weinberg, a researcher and expert on health care reform for the nonpartisan New America Foundation, "American businesses—large and small—are being hamstrung by soaring health care costs that are more than *twice* those of foreign competitors." *Twice?* America can compete in a global economy, but the days have long passed when we could afford to spot every competitor that many points.

As far back as 2005 General Motors was spending more on health care costs (over $1,500) per car than on steel! That's an unreal advantage to foreign carmakers. Didn't anyone see this coming?

The brilliant Bill Clinton, who has an uncanny way of cutting to the heart of the issue, told Jon Meacham in a 2009 *Newsweek* interview that the difference between what the United States spends in GDP (17 percent) on health care and what other industrialized nations spend, the average 6 percent difference, amounts to giving them a $900 billion competitive advantage!

It should be so simple, yet some conservatives are so dug into their dogma that they can't see that the policies they support are the ones killing the free market and the independent businesses they claim to revere.

UNCHECKED CAPITALISM CREATES NEGATIVE SOCIALIST OUTCOMES

Between 2000 and 2007, the average worker's insurance premiums grew *twice as fast as his or her wages.* During the same time frame, according to Joseph Antos of the American Enterprise Institute in Washington, premiums for employer-sponsored insurance jumped 98 percent—four times faster than wages.

This employee-based system has led to workers chasing benefits from job to job, not necessarily doing what they love or are particularly good at. Common sense tells us that this is no way for any society to thrive. Think about it. Poorly regulated capitalism has forced Americans into jobs for which they are ill suited, which is one of the great fears people have of socialism. Paradoxically, if we free workers from taking jobs based on whether or not that job provides health care, we strengthen capitalism because we encourage people to do what they are best suited to do.

CAREENING TOWARD INSOLVENCY

"You can't fix the economy without fixing health care," President Obama has said. While I have been critical of the White House strategy on health care reform, I do understand what an incredibly difficult lift this is. Had he not inherited such a wretched economy and massive debt, President Obama could have passed much more substantial legislation because he would have had the money in the bank to make the initial investments. Instead, he had to settle for reforms that were immediately budget neutral or that promised savings. Had Bush II been held to that standard,

Medicare Part D, which Republicans passed despite its $1.2 trillion price tag (over ten years), would have been sunk. As it was, the unfunded plan floated away in a sea of red ink. Because Bush wrote all those hot checks then, average American families are paying the price now.

Before the Democrats took on health care reform, the New America Foundation projected that health insurance in 2016 could cost $20,400 annually for a family. Some will say if we are paying anything less than that in 2016, it is a victory. If so, it's a small victory, and I don't plan any kind of celebration in the end zone. The tiresome term used during the health care debate was that proponents wanted to "bend the curve" on costs—in other words, tamp down the *pace* of the increases.

The reality is, even with the consumer protections in any new health care legislation, there just isn't enough leverage to bring about any kind of immediate relief for most people. Families will probably still see their costs rise—but at a slower rate than had this runaway train been allowed to keep rolling. Under the proposed legislation under consideration as this book went to press, Americans will no longer be denied coverage, but what we don't know is how high rates will go. Can we expect real competition? Will we finally have a country in which getting sick doesn't mean financial ruin? Folks, it's too early to tell.

According to a Harvard and Ohio University study in 2007, medical-related expenses triggered almost two thirds of all bankruptcies in the United States that year, a 50 percent increase from 2001. "Our findings are frightening. Unless you're Warren Buffett, your family is just one serious illness away from bankruptcy," lead author Dr. David Himmelstein, an associate professor of medicine at Harvard Medical School, said in a news release.

Dr. Steffie Woolhandler, an associate professor of medicine at Harvard Medical School and coauthor of the Harvard and Ohio University study, said, "Only single-payer national health insurance can make universal, comprehensive coverage affordable by saving the hundreds of billions we now waste on insurance overhead and bureaucracy."

Sadly, as the health care debate unfolded, we could see that most Republicans and some Democrats—enough to screw things up—were more concerned with the health of health insurance companies than they were about American workers.

Here was the response of Representative Eric Cantor (R-VA) in a town hall meeting after hearing about a woman who had recently lost her job and her insurance and then discovered that she had stomach cancer: He encouraged her to look to "existing government programs" or "charitable organizations." Maybe she could get a tin cup and beg on the streets.

Representative Alan Grayson (D-FL) said sarcastically during a speech on the House floor, "Don't get sick. If you get sick, America, the Republican health care plan is this: Die quickly." The failure of health care reform to cover everyone does kill, and the sad thing about the new health care legislation is that it will not cover some 23 million Americans.

A family that falls between the cracks and is living hand to mouth in a tough economy can't afford cancer screening. Too many people wait too long for treatment because they cannot afford it. How many victims of our for-profit health care system will we accept before we finally do the right thing and embrace universal care?

Think about this: During the past eight years, there's been about a *428 percent increase in profits* for the insurance industry giants, while middle-class families have been getting financially butchered—and the Republicans want to blame big government!

This is not America.

This is not the country I grew up in.

Fairness left the building with Elvis.

SO MANY PILLS, SO MANY DOLLARS

Let's take a look at the whole way we approach pharmaceuticals. Lobbyists have fixed the game against American consumers. Nowhere is the fix more blatant than in the Bush Medicare prescription plan for seniors.

The law is specifically written to deny the government the right to negotiate prices. Tell me, is that capitalism or theft?

Pharmaceutical prices are much higher in America than around the
world because American drug companies charge what they can get
away with—and they can get away with a lot. In fact, with health care
legislation brewing, drugmakers raised their prices more than *9 percent*
in 2009, according to the *New York Times*. In that story, Harvard health
economist Joseph P. Newhouse said he found a similar pattern of unusual price increases after Congress added drug benefits to Medicare:
"Just as the program was taking effect in 2006, the drug industry raised
prices by the widest margin in a half-dozen years."

In countries with some kind of socialized medicine, such as Canada,
the government negotiates drug prices. Senator Byron Dorgan (D-ND)
offered an amendment to the health care bill to allow Americans to buy
prescription drugs from Canada, but it was quashed. He says, "The Lipitor that is sold in Canada is *one half* the price of the identical bottle of
Lipitor purchased in the U.S. by American consumers. And the same is
true for most of the brand name prescription drugs."

The simple solution, according to Senator Dorgan, is allowing the
American consumer to take advantage of the global economy. "I'm talking about allowing FDA approved drugs produced in FDA approved
plants overseas," Dorgan says. "The same pill put in the same bottle.
How can that be unsafe?"

MEDICAL TOURISM—OUTSOURCING SURGERY

People have always traveled to other countries for medical procedures,
but in some cases today—it's sad to say—traveling to another country
may be the most affordable (and so, sometimes, the only) option. In many
places, the quality of care and outcomes are equal to or better than our
own. Heart bypass surgery, easily a $100,000 procedure here, costs
$12,000 in Thailand. A $25,000 hip replacement in the United States can

be done in India for a fourth of the cost. As long as we are unable to lower medical costs for Americans, "medical tourism" is going to be part of the answer to our health care crisis.

Of course, even this is affordable only to the upper middle class. It's wonderful to have the option of having your dental surgery done on a tropical island, but what a sad state of affairs to realize that in the richest nation on earth, some citizens must travel to other countries for humane and affordable medical treatment. If you can't afford the price of a plane ticket, I guess you just endure.

OTHER COMMONSENSE STEPS
TO A HEALTHIER AMERICA

We need to attack this health care crisis on all fronts. For one thing, we need a national focus and program on fitness, starting with our schools. Physical fitness is not the priority it needs to be. Today's kids are not as active as previous generations. Heck, if I had owned an Xbox 360, my butt might have been parked in front of it, too. But it wasn't an option. We played baseball and football in the neighborhood. If we make a commitment to physical activity and education in our schools, it will make a dramatic difference down the line. Our kids will be healthier, live longer, and pay less for health care as they age.

I know health insurance companies "grade" individuals based on age, weight, and other benchmarks to arrive at a premium price. I wonder, though, if we could implement a system of rewards for those who take part in exercise programs or adapt other measurable lifestyle changes. The idea is to give the consumer a real say in lowering the cost of insurance. I know this is an idea big businesses have been successful with— rewarding employees for lifestyle changes, which means healthier employees and fewer sick days. It also saves the company money.

The *Wall Street Journal* reports, "Syngenta's U.S. staffers collect as much as $250 a year for taking part in annual health-risk assessments, exercise classes and similar wellness activities. When officials distributed T-shirts to introduce the program in 1998, obesity was so widespread that they ordered many sized XXXL. Syngenta said the [wellness] program helped lower its average annual health-care inflation to 8.9% between 2005 and 2008. That's less than the 9.7% average annual rate for all U.S. employers." The company included spouses in the programs after discovering that spouses' claims exceeded those of employees by 30 percent.

Can we apply some broad criteria—a national wellness program—so that small businesses and individual policyholders can reap similar rewards? What a marvelous way of encouraging fitness and saving. A national wellness program will save trillions in generations to come and may be the finest legacy we pass on to our children and grandchildren.

And we need to stop protecting the tobacco industry and allowing them to purposely make their cigarettes more addicting than heroin. I'm not ready to ban tobacco or coffee or, for heaven's sakes, a cool one after eighteen holes, but this insidious practice of purposely making a product addictive, which they do, is immoral, and those predators need to be shut down *yesterday*.

What they do is add ammonia, which allows more efficient absorption of nicotine. In a Pulitzer Prize–winning exposé in 1995, the *Wall Street Journal* reported: "Ammonia increases 'impact' says Neil Benowitz, a professor and nicotine-research specialist at the University of California in San Francisco, because 'the faster nicotine is absorbed, the more reinforcing or satisfying it is and the greater its psychological effect.'"

These people ought to be locked up.

Our approach to tobacco is pretty convoluted. Americans subsidized tobacco farmers $530 million between 1995 and 2006. (I can see subsidies for food, but for a product that causes so much misery, are you kidding me?) Meanwhile, federal and state governments spend millions more to stop people from using tobacco—Florida alone spent $58 million in 2009 on such efforts.

How many lives could we save, imagine the boon to productivity, if we could beat cancer, stroke, autism, Alzheimer's, heart disease, and diabetes? The National Cancer Institute was budgeted to get $4.8 billion in 2009. The Department of Defense—$515 billion. Cancer kills 560,000 Americans each year. Heart disease kills 650,000. That's 1.2 million deaths a year. In comparison, there have been about 1.3 million American fatalities in all the wars America has *ever* fought.

It's a matter of perspective and priority.

Surely a Manhattan Project to cure these diseases is in order. Let's ramp up stem cell research, too. The hypocrisy of George W. Bush and his cronies effectively stalling stem cell advances for his two terms infuriates me. How much closer could we be to a breakthrough that would cure leukemia and other blood disorders if Bush hadn't stalled us? How far away has this put us from literally growing the organs for transplants that could save so many lives?

But if we socialize medicine, won't medical research—deprived of big pharma investment—stop dead in its tracks? Of course not; that kind of thinking sells our basic humanity short. There are always people motivated to make the world a better place. I'd like to think it's in everyone's DNA—except maybe Dick Cheney's. When Jonas Salk discovered an inoculation against polio, he refused to patent and profit from his years of research. When asked once who owned the patent, Salk replied, "There is no patent. Could you patent the sun?" We certainly should find a way to reward medical advancements handsomely, but we ought to be able to do so without holding sick people hostage to the high cost of new drugs and technology.

Perhaps we need to examine the funding relationship between private pharmaceutical companies and the government. The relationship has merit—certainly there have been some remarkable advances—but why haven't we licked cancer yet? Meanwhile, we have a number of remedies for erectile dysfunction. Hey, I'm all for good wood, but doesn't it suggest that maybe our priorities get skewed when the potential for profit gets involved?

It took us decades to get in this health care mess and maybe it is unrealistic to expect to change overnight. We lost an entire generation and a golden opportunity under the Clinton administration. You can place the blame for that one right at the feet of the Republican Party.

What was even more ironic about the way the Republicans destroyed our chance for health care reform that time was that the Clinton plan was almost a mirror image of one proposed in 1974 by President Richard Nixon, who called for universal health care in his final State of the Union address. According to a 2007 report in McClatchy newspapers, "Nixon first proposed national health insurance as a conservative California congressman in 1947. He grew up poor and lost two brothers to tuberculosis, which marked him for life. He frequently pointed to the cure for tuberculosis as a medical marvel that underscored the need for a public-private partnership on health care."

Of course, with Watergate coming to a boil, Nixon's dream of universal coverage faded. His successor, Gerald Ford, abandoned the idea when the economy went south. And that has been the story—we just keep pushing our problems down the tracks—and the price tag keeps getting higher every day.

In reality, there is no free health care. There is no free anything. At some level, we all must contribute. The emerging model of health care reform mandates that Americans buy insurance. That isn't new. We pay for Social Security and Medicare. What is different is that we are being forced to buy a product from private industry. I wrestle with that. It's a sticky, possibly unconstitutional issue.

We all understand that there is a price to citizenship, but I would feel a whole lot better if my mandated payment went to my government for universal coverage rather than to a proven den of vipers in the health insurance industry.

NATIONAL HEALTH CARE IS THE MONEY SMART SOLUTION

Anything less than a national single-payer option is like using Band-Aids on a sucking chest wound. It'll end up wasting more time and more money.

The next baby step is the public option, a *viable* government competitor to existing health care insurers. If that happens, two things are possible: One, health insurers will slowly go out of business or find niche roles as they do in Singapore and other countries with government health care, or two, they will do what they should have done long ago, get efficient, get competitive, and for God's sake, get some ethics.

If government health care is as inefficient as the ideologues say, there should be nothing to fear from a government option. People will choose the best product. It's not like we're reinventing the wheel here. According to a 2009 report from the nonpartisan New America Foundation, "There are many examples of public and private insurance plans peacefully coexisting. More than 30 state governments . . . offer their employees a choice between traditional private health insurance products and a plan that the state insures. In Washington State, for example, the publicly insured option called the Uniform Medical Plan is the most popular choice, but about a third of public employees choose a private plan instead."

And Medicare, a government program, works. Again, no one wants to say much about this, but I will. Yes, I trust my government with health care. I don't expect it to be perfect, but I expect it to be more efficient than private insurance. It's a well-established fact that 3 percent of every Medicare dollar is spent on administration compared to 13 percent and higher with private plans. What if doctors only had to contend with paperwork from one insurer? Instead, we pay paper pushers to deal with fifteen hundred insurers with different forms and requirements. Going to a single-payer system would save $350 billion a year, according to Physicians for a National Health Program.

A friend of mine who worked in the medical industry argued that a single-payer system would mean fewer people entering the field, because they wouldn't make as much money. My answer? If people are becoming doctors just to become rich, they're part of the problem. I want a healer—not a businessman. That said, I want my doctors to be fairly compensated. We certainly cannot expect them to come out of medical school owing hundreds of thousands of dollars and then work for minimum wage—which brings me back to my belief that education has to be accessible and affordable (ideally, a right of citizenship) for everyone. In any case, I have no doubt that good people will still go into medicine when we have a national health care system. Smart, caring people still become doctors in Sweden and in France; nationalizing health care doesn't stop people from loving medicine and wanting to excel in that field.

AND, YES, IT'S ALSO TIME FOR TORT REFORM

While I do believe there has to be legal recourse for malpractice, the insurance premiums doctors are paying are oppressive, ranging as high as $200,000 a year. I support tort reform—changes in the civil justice system that would reduce a doctor's liability in the case of medical malpractice—because I believe it is part of the ultimate solution to reducing health care costs. According to a 2008 report by Dr. Michael Lynch in the *Concord Monitor,* medical malpractice premiums have gone up 50 percent in five years.

According to the Associated Press, malpractice lawsuits alone add about $6 billion annually to the cost of health care. The Congressional

Budget Office found in 2009 that the cost of malpractice insurance *and* lawsuits accounts for about 2 percent of health care costs—about $35 billion. Placed in context with the overall cost of our national health care system, $2.4 trillion, it isn't much, but the threat of lawsuits alone influences costs. It causes doctors to order battery after battery of unnecessary tests to avoid accusations of malpractice. The insurance company pays more, premiums rise . . . and well, you can see how prices begin to spiral out of control.

I can understand a physician's frustration at being treated like the enemy when something goes wrong. We have to understand that there are so many variables and uncertainties that sometimes patients just don't make it. If there is gross negligence, all right then: Consider a lawsuit. But we have to create an environment in which physicians don't have to feel as if they are always working with the Sword of Damocles over their heads.

TACTICIANS AND DREAMERS

There were two provisions in the new health care legislation that were made to placate Republicans. One was that abortions would not be funded under the program and the other was that illegal aliens would not be covered. Well, the notion that anyone with a sucking chest wound is going to be left to die on the emergency room steps is complete fiction. And are we really going to inoculate only American citizens and leave a large segment of the population unprotected, spreading disease? The last time I checked, the H1N1 virus was unable to distinguish between documented and undocumented workers. What if something far more serious began to spread? This is a dangerous political game.

I want to find one senator or congressperson who will look me in the eye and tell me first of all that this is plausible, let alone workable. It's fiction—a bullshit fairy tale for the American public to make them feel better. At some point, someone is going to have to run the numbers through the Congressional Budget Office on this issue. We may actually save money by including illegal immigrants in the program rather than limiting them to high-priced emergency care.

During the debate over health care, many members of the House and Senate acted like ostriches. They were willing to run to the CBO to make sure the bill saved money, but no one wanted to ask the CBO how real universal health care would pencil out. They didn't ask because they were afraid of the answer. I am going to get behind legislation to make the ostrich the national bird—it will be perfect for this crowd.

Given a credible universal health care proposal, the CBO might well have discovered it to be cheaper than the present system. Americans would have been marching in the streets demanding it, and Congress would have been faced with a choice between doing what was right for the health care industry or for the American people. That's like asking Archie to choose between Betty and Veronica. Who to choose? If you are a politician, the chances are you're going to pick Veronica—the rich girl.

Senator Max Baucus (D-MT), chairman of the Senate Finance Committee, made every effort to ram through a watered-down health care bill that to me looked like a giant suck-up to the health care industry. This is a guy who had raised nearly $12 million in five years for his re-election efforts. Let me tell you, that kind of money doesn't come from Billings, Montana. According to the *Washington Post,* "Baucus collected $3 million from the health and insurance sectors from 2003 to 2008. . . . Less than 10 percent of the money came from Montana."

The *Washington Post* story continues: "Craig Holman, government affairs lobbyist for the Public Citizen advocacy group, said the *continued* fundraising by Baucus during the health-care debate is very troubling. 'He's doing all this fundraising right in the middle of this effort to mark up a bill,' Holman said. 'When you put these events close to matters concerning these lobbyists, clearly it's a signal. You are expected to show up with a check.'"

This begs the question: Who is Max Baucus looking out for? There are plenty of similar examples. In 2008 the Senate Finance Committee members received a total of $13,263,986 from health care industries. Do you think that influenced the process? According to the Center for Responsive Politics, the health care sector gave almost $170 million to federal lawmakers in 2007 and 2008, 54 percent of that amount going to Democrats.

Senator Charles "Don't Pull the Plug on Grandma" Grassley, an Iowa Republican, has received a cool $2 million from the health care and insurance industries since 2003. Grassley, a big supporter of the Medicare Part D boondoggle, apparently was good with end-of-life counseling when it was included in that bill!

Senator Joe Lieberman, the erstwhile independent from Connecticut, has pocketed $1.5 million in donations from the health care and insurance sector since 2003. This guy has the world's biggest ego matched with the world's smallest conscience—in short, the perfect politician. Two industries will make a mint off of Lieberman's cronyism and health care obstructionism—the insurance companies and the shoe repair shop that will replace all the heels Lieberman ruined from digging in against anything that might constitute a break for the American family. The only good thing about Bush II winning in 2000 was that it kept Joe Lieberman's wrinkly ass out of the vice president's office.

According to OpenSecrets.org data, Senator Blanche Lincoln, the Arkansas Democrat who helped shoot down a public insurance option—a huge favor to her friends at Blue Cross–Blue Shield—received more than three quarters of a million dollars from the health and insurance industry in the last five years. BCBS dominates 75 percent of the market in Arkansas. Lincoln is also a friend of Walmart, and predictably she opposes the Employee Free Choice Act, which would make it easier to form unions.

With Democrats like that, who needs Republicans?

And let's not forget another politician who helped throttle meaningful health care, Senator Mary Landrieu, a Louisiana Democrat, who has been showered with nearly $1.7 million from the health care and insurance industries during the course of her federal career. She famously received $100 million for her state—another Louisiana Purchase—in exchange for not stalling the health care process.

Both Landrieu and Lincoln have former staffers who are high-powered lobbyists for health care and insurance interests. Are you beginning to see how this works?

We have met the enemy, and some of them are us. Take Senator Ben Nelson (D-NE), who insisted his state receive special Medicare funding before he would vote for health care reform. In the end he was shamed into backing down. Campaignmoney.org, the website of the Public Campaign Action Fund, notes, "Nelson spent his career as an insurance executive, insurance company lawyer and, early in his career, Nebraska's state insurance regulator. He was chief executive officer of an insurance company and has sided with and received political support from business groups opposed to a public health plan as part of health reform." The Center for Responsive Politics (OpenSecrets.org) reports that Nelson has received more than $2 million from insurance and health care interests in three campaigns for federal office.

I was especially disappointed in Senator Kent Conrad (D-ND), a member of the Senate Finance Committee and a longtime friend, for not supporting a public option. During his career, according to the Center for Responsive Politics, he has received in campaign donations more than $828,000 from insurance companies, $610,000 from health professionals, and $255,000 from pharmaceutical and health product companies. I know he thinks that health insurance co-ops can make a difference and that he didn't have the votes for a public option, but there is a time to attempt the impossible. This is a guy who, at the age of thirty-eight, achieved the impossible in 1986 by knocking off a favored incumbent, Mark Andrews, who had been in Washington since 1963! Until it was settled, no one thought he had the votes then either, but he had a slim 2,100-vote margin. That's all it took to win. When he went to the U.S.

Senate, he pledged to help balance the budget or come home. Well, he did neither, but I thought he was a terrific senator who just overestimated the task and the times ahead. I loved the audacious Kent Conrad who dared to dream big.

This health care debate was another opportunity to dream big, but that big-dreaming Kent Conrad was absent from the debate, replaced by just another political tactician. No one in Washington understands the budget better than Kent Conrad, and few senators work harder than he does. He's learned a lot in Washington, but I fear Kent Conrad has forgotten how to dream. Regretfully, he is not the only one.

Perhaps it has become politically passé to dream, but that's what Barack Obama sold us, and that is what inspired Conrad to endorse Obama—one of the first senators to do so. What happened to the dream? Where are the dreamers? Are forty Senate Republicans that damn tough?

At times like this, I hear in my mind the words of another dreamer, Senator Robert Kennedy, who said, "There are those who look at things the way they are, and ask why? . . . I dream of things that never were, and ask why not?"

Why not? The only thing stopping us from accomplishing big things is that we have forgotten how to dream big.

IT'S GOING TO TAKE TIME

In the future, generations will be astonished that health care was ever considered anything but an inalienable right. Until then, we have work to do. What's it going to take to get to this promised land? It may well take a movement for a basic human right like the one led so majestically by Martin Luther King.

When I said this to Stephen A. Smith, the *Philadelphia Inquirer* columnist and one of my favorite guest commentators, he said the health care issue was *even bigger* than that because that cause was about African-Americans. This one is about *everyone*. This isn't an issue of politics or capitalism versus socialism or even dollars and cents. This speaks to who we are as a country and who we aspire to be.

The pragmatist in me can accept that change may take longer than the idealist in me wants to accept. The goal is to lower the cost for consumers to an affordable or sustainable level. And we have to realize that at some level we all pay for the services we receive as citizens of this country. I just happen to believe universal health care is the best alternative.

What is so hard about doing the right thing?

I know we're better than this.

We have to be.

CHAPTER FOUR

RETHINKING ENERGY

Another Fight for Independence

I CAN'T HELP BUT THINK ABOUT THE FUTURE. NOT MINE SO MUCH, but the world we are leaving the next generation—my kids and yours. As I said earlier in this book, one of the handicaps of a democratic society is that our political and corporate leaders tend to think in election cycles and in quarters, not in a generational context. We don't address growing problems until they become a crisis. *Then* we muster the will to change. But that way of doing things can be much more painful than it has to be. The issues that are looming before us are not the ones that should divide us. It's not about gays, guns, and God. Those are social issues manufactured to get votes. The real issues coming down the pike affect us all and in a big way.

What if it were possible to rise above partisan politics, to bring both parties together, to find common ground and common goals? What if we were able to set out *national goals* that most of us could agree upon? We could seek a balanced budget in five years. Reduce cancer deaths by 75 percent in ten years . . . energy independence in ten years . . . Really, the sky is the limit if we could get a bipartisan think tank of politicians and others from the private sector to take on these key issues.

Let's talk about energy. I said in a previous chapter that we all pay taxes that subsidize military involvement in getting oil from the Middle East. One estimate is that our actual cost per gallon of gas is closer to $10. Our latest incursion in Iraq may eventually cost us $3 trillion, according to economist Joseph E. Stiglitz, yet consumers didn't save money. Prices at the pump hit $4 a gallon on Bush's watch. The American taxpayer got it coming and going.

America imports 70 percent of its oil—somewhere around 10 million barrels per day. About 5.5 million barrels a day comes from OPEC (Organization of the Petroleum Exporting Countries) nations. Most of the balance comes from Canada and Mexico. Ominously, according to Merrill Lynch, non-OPEC production has probably peaked to about 49–50 million barrels a day, and could slide to 47 million barrels a day by 2015. OPEC, which closely manages output, has been pumping around 30 million barrels a day.

In the immediate future, petroleum is going to continue to play a big part in the energy picture. As a country, we are addicted to oil, much as a junkie is addicted to heroin. The difference is, when he knocks down someone's door to feed his habit, the junkie doesn't have an army. (Please, let's not even argue the point that our interest in Iraq was about oil. If our goals were humanitarian, we would have been in Somolia, but their main cash crop is bananas, and we're not addicted to bananas.)

The problem is not just our junkie-like behavior; it is that there is another energy junkie in the neighborhood with a growing habit—China, which consumes about 7 million barrels a day and is getting thirstier by the minute.

For the first time in history, in 2009, Chinese domestic auto sales exceeded those of the United States. All of those vehicles are going to be burning gasoline.

Competition for oil forces prices upward, as it does any commodity. That's exacerbated by speculation and market manipulation. But while the global thirst for oil is on the rise, most experts say production has peaked.

I don't know what happens when two desperate junkies are in the same room with the last needle full of smack, but I can predict what will happen if China and the United States get to that point. Geopolitics is one giant chess game, with countries continually positioning themselves to their best advantage. When it comes to the politics of oil, a finite resource, that chess game has already been lost. No one is going to win, but the longer we play, the better chance there is that the board will be overturned as fists begin flying. Both our economic and ecological salvation rests in our ability to go green.

Getting more than half of our oil from OPEC is not a good business plan. These people are not our friends. In 1973, they turned the spigot off and sent shock waves through our economy, though we were only importing 15 percent of our oil from OPEC then as compared to *more than half today.*

First things first—let's stop doing business with OPEC as soon as possible by conserving, developing alternative energy sources, and producing more domestically. Because petroleum is used to make so many things—imagine if every bit of plastic suddenly disappeared from your home—it will play a role in our foreseeable future.

To wean ourselves from oil, we have to conserve, become more efficient, produce more, or simply do without. It's important that we subsidize alternative energies when necessary to ensure they have a fighting chance economically against the existing petro-economy, which, as I have noted, is surreptitiously underwritten by the muscle of the U.S. military. Ultimately, though, new technology has to make sense to the marketplace while meeting pollution standards. One thing we know for certain: The petroleum-based economy is a dead-end street. There is a limited supply and the damage to our environment has us at an ecological tipping point. So it makes sense for us to conserve and be more efficient before we try to drill our way out of trouble.

What about "Drill, baby, drill"? Well, it's dumb, baby, dumb to think we're going to drill our way out of this. It's simple math. We don't have the domestic reserves to support our habit. Yeah, but what about Alaska? According to the Department of Energy, "there is a 95 percent probability that at least 5.7 billion barrels of oil may be technically recoverable from the ANWR Coastal Plain of the Alaska North Slope." *Peak* production is estimated at 650,000 barrels per day. It's hard for me to conceive that such a relatively small amount can have any impact—except on the pocketbooks of oil companies running out the string.

I'm not saying we should abandon drilling, but we ought to transition to renewable energy. President Bush lifted the drilling ban on coastal waters that are believed to contain 18 billion barrels of oil and 76 trillion cubic feet of natural gas, based on seismic surveys in the late 1970s and early 1980s. Drilling is necessary during our transition away from OPEC oil and to green energy, but it is just part of the solution.

IT ALL STARTS WITH CONSERVATION

Since 61 percent of the oil we consume globally is for transportation, according to the Global Market Information Database (2007), we need to start there. I know Americans have a love affair with the car, but some things are going to have to change. Even as I write, automakers are shifting gears to electric cars. The Chevrolet Volt, expected to cost around $40,000, will get about 230 miles per gallon with a forty-mile range. The Department of Transportation says eight out of ten drivers commute less than forty miles a day, so it stands to reason that such vehicles could have a positive impact very quickly.

For years, Wendy and I have driven an electric GEM car at our lake home in Minnesota. It's like a large golf cart and perfect for scooting short distances. We love it. Plus, it's built in Fargo, North Dakota, and we like to support our local industries.

But ultimately electric cars will have to achieve the range of gasoline-powered vehicles. One key is battery technology. It's an old technology, but improving it is crucial not only to extending the potential reach of an electric car, but also for changing the way we produce and consume electricity. I don't think any one technology alone will free us from the petroleum habit, but the ability to store the power we create makes sense.

Another one of the goals of the Obama administration is to make the existing electric grid, which is susceptible to cascading blackouts, more efficient. There are actually three power grids operating in the forty-eight contiguous states—one east of the Rocky Mountains, another from the Pacific Ocean to the Rocky Mountain states, and the third the Texas Interconnected System.

In 2003 there was a giant blackout in the Northeast encompassing Cleveland, Toronto, Detroit, New York City, and thousands of communities in between. Traffic signals went dark. Subways stopped. People were stuck in elevators. Thousands were forced to walk across the Brooklyn Bridge. The outage persisted for days in some places, costing an estimated $6 billion in economic losses, according to the Department of Energy. It turns out the problem originated with an Ohio power company. Overgrown trees had come into contact with power lines.

Not only is our grid susceptible to something as seemingly benign as overgrown trees, security experts believe that the system is wide open to cyber attack. In 2009 the *Wall Street Journal* reported that the Chinese and the Russians have infiltrated the grid and could take it out in the event of a war. Intelligence officials say cyber-spies have accessed systems operating everything from financial institutions to sewage. Obviously, these vulnerabilities need to be eliminated.

A new "smart grid" promises to address a very inefficient system. Computer technology can help direct energy where it is needed. By providing instant feedback to customers through meters in their homes that will tell how much energy their appliances are using and the current cost, power companies will enable consumers to choose to use energy when demand is low and the price is cheaper. If you do laundry when demand is low, you can save. Brilliant in its simplicity!

Other advances include the use of high-temperature superconductors to provide loss-less transmission of electrical power by using liquid nitrogen to keep the lines cool. That's important to the energy market because often power generated hundreds of miles away is cheaper than a more local source.

While technology and other infrastructure investments should help us use electricity more efficiently on the grid, I believe that it can also make communities and individual households less dependent on it. I think the natural process will be for homeowners to seek energy independence from the grid through wind and solar power. It's *Back to the Future*. . . . In rural America, before electric cooperatives energized farms, folks depended on generators and wind for power. Some systems involved batteries, which were charged by wind generators.

Once again, we are seeing wind farms spring up.

North Dakota has been called the Saudi Arabia of wind energy, and it is just one of many states that are poised to become big wind energy players. However, at the moment, we lack the infrastructure to really capitalize on this source. According to the Department of Energy, "while electricity demand increased by about 25 percent since 1990, construction of transmission facilities decreased about 30 percent. In fact, annual investment in new transmission facilities has declined over the last 25 years."

That hasn't stopped companies from investing in niche areas where there is both wind and available transmission line capacity. In windy regions, companies are competing hard to lease land for towers, just as they do in oil countries before they sink wells. When large capacity lines are built, the wind industry will be able to shoulder a significant portion of our country's energy needs.

SCIENCE WILL LEAD THE WAY

It's hard to imagine where this necessary transition away from fossil fuels will lead and how it will transform the world. Will we use more natural gas in coming decades or will hydrogen fuel technology come on line sooner than we think? Perhaps we will become so proficient at creating solar and wind energy—and storing it—that it will become the dominant energy source. The answers to these questions all depend upon the ingenuity of scientific minds—and on the market.

I'm optimistic and excited. I think green energy will be a major turning point in man's evolution and that we are living on the cusp of that transition. The sooner we embrace the transition, the more hope I have. It's an exciting time. Booms and busts relate closely to the cost of energy. Cheap energy drives progress. Our ability to create affordable alternative energy will have a lot to say about whether the Great American Boom is over or just moving into a new green phase.

In an op-ed for the *New York Times* after Obama's election, Al Gore said, "Here is the good news. The bold steps that are needed to solve the climate crisis are exactly the same steps that ought to be taken in order to solve the economic crisis and the energy security crisis. Economists across the spectrum—including Martin Feldstein and Lawrence Summers—agree that large and rapid investment in a jobs-intensive infrastructure initiative is the best way to revive our economy in a quick and sustainable way. Many also agree that our economy will fall behind if we continue spending hundreds of billions of dollars on foreign oil every year. Moreover, national security experts in both parties agree that we face a dangerous strategic vulnerability if the world suddenly loses access to Middle Eastern oil."

WHAT ABOUT COAL?

Statistics from the Energy Information Administration show that "coal-fired plants contribute 45.4 percent of the nation's electric power. Nuclear plants contribute 21.0 percent, while 20.8 percent is generated at natural gas–fired plants. Of the 1.2 percent generated by petroleum-fired plants, petroleum liquids represented 0.8 percent, with the remainder from petroleum coke. Conventional hydroelectric power provides 7.5 percent of the total, while other renewables (biomass, geothermal, solar, and wind) and other miscellaneous energy sources account for the remaining 4.2 percent of electric power."

I come from coal country. North Dakota is a major coal-powered energy producer. It's cheap and abundant, but as a global industry, there are real drawbacks. The Sierra Club says, "Power plants are a major source of air pollution, with coal-fired power plants spewing 59 percent of total U.S. sulfur dioxide pollution and 18 percent of total nitrogen oxides every year. Coal-fired power plants are also the largest polluter of toxic mercury pollution, largest contributor of hazardous air toxics, and release about 50 percent of particle pollution."

According to the Sierra Club, power plant pollution is responsible for thirty thousand deaths each year. Additionally, power plants release over 40 percent of total U.S. carbon dioxide emissions, a prime contributor to climate change.

I have friends and supporters in the coal industry, so I have a personal interest in seeing the industry come up with a viable solution to CO_2 emissions. If we can do so, coal deposits in America are so vast we could become energy independent. But we are in the race of our lives. Scientists tell us if we do not begin reducing greenhouse gases now, climate change has the potential to dramatically and negatively change the way we live, to the point of a planet-wide catastrophe.

But seemingly, profit trumps even the potential for global disaster, and the race is on to see how many power plants can be built before new regulations go into effect. As I write this in 2009, forty-three coal-fired plants are under construction to be "grandfathered in" before stringent new regulations go into effect requiring new plants to sequester half of their CO_2 emissions. Up to now in this decade 5,600 MW of new coal-fired electric power have been added to the grid. The forty-three new plants will quadruple that—and produce more than 150 million tons of new CO_2 emissions every year. That's just wrong.

Here, again, is an illustration of how the corporate me-first greedy mentality fails to discern the difference between what is legal and what is moral. It is a symptom of what has gone so terribly wrong in America— we've learned to justify greed.

It isn't the first time that the good intentions of lawmakers have been counterproductive. Ironically, the 1970 Clean Air Act, while regulating many pollutants, did not address CO_2 because no one was talking about climate change then. The Clean Air Act controlled particulates and sulfur, but in order to implement this new, cleaner technology, coal power companies became less efficient and as a consequence sent *more* CO_2 into the atmosphere.

One of the most promising solutions anyone has come up with is to inject coal plant carbon dioxide back into the earth. Basin Electric Power Cooperative in North Dakota captures half of its CO_2 when it processes coal into natural gas. The revolutionary coal gasification project cost $1.5 billion in the 1980s. However, to replicate it today would cost an estimated $4 billion.

Duke Energy CEO Jim Rogers told *60 Minutes,* "What we need in this country is what I would call a Marshall Plan. We rebuilt the economies of Japan and Germany after World War II. We need to rebuild our economy and transition it to a low carbon economy. We can do that. But it's gonna take trillions of dollars to do it."

OTHER OPTIONS

I have been supportive of the ethanol industry because I believe it has the potential to play a role in energy independence. I see it as an evolving technology—away from corn and to cellulose—but it may prove to be transitional and nothing more if electric cars improve enough or if hydrogen fuel cells become a reality. Toyota has plans to build a hydrogen-powered car by 2015. Even if it's successful, the prospects for the new technology rest upon the construction of "hydrogen stations" across the country like there are gas stations.

It is no surprise that the fossil fuel industry is lobbying hard against any legislation that will help green energy become more competitive. With them, it's all about business, and they have a whole battalion of scientists who will tell you what you want to hear. But green energy *is* getting more competitive, and clean energy will win in the end. *Electronic Business* reports that soon "leading solar electricity providers in Spain will be able to produce solar electricity for as low as 10 cents per kilowatt-hour (kWh)—equivalent to the delivered cost of electricity from a new coal power plant."

If that is so, and that kind of efficiency can be replicated, it will impact the coal and nuclear industries. Naturally, when we start talking about energy, people come out of the woodwork in support of nuclear power. However, in a recent study, Amory B. Lovins and Imran Sheikh compared the cost from a new nuclear plant at 14¢ per kilowatt hour with that of a wind farm—7¢ per kilowatt hour. The study did not even address the costs of disposing of the nuclear waste. The government plan has been to store the deadly stuff underground at Yucca Mountain in Nevada. Quite naturally, citizens in the state are against it.

I don't see nuclear energy as a smart play—the risks are too great. Remember Chernobyl? It laid waste to land twice the size of South Carolina. But continuing to churn out greenhouse gases could be even more catastrophic.

GLOBAL WARMING OR MAYBE A NEW ICE AGE?

According to an Associated Press report after the 2009 Copenhagen international summit on climate change, leaders aim to cap carbon dioxide at 450 parts per million, which would concede an increase in the global temperature of 2.3 degrees Fahrenheit. We're at 390 ppm now. The report quotes NASA scientist Cynthia Rosenweig, who says going above 450 ppm "will change everything," adding, "It's not just one or two things. There will be changes in water, food, ecosystems, health, and those changes also interact with each other." She warns about coastal flooding, droughts, the death of coral reefs, and a chain reaction that would affect the food chain. Twenty percent of the world's known species would be endangered.

Scientists warn that we are approaching a point of no return when global warming will melt the Arctic permafrost, releasing even more CO_2, triggering a cascade of events that will be irreversible.

You'll get similarly dire predictions from the Sierra Club and even our own stodgy EPA. The Sierra Club notes, "Average global temperatures have risen already by one degree Fahrenheit, and projections indicate an increase of *two to ten degrees* within this century" (emphasis mine). The EPA warns, "Increased greenhouse gas concentrations are very likely to raise the Earth's average temperature, influence precipitation and some storm patterns, as well as raise sea levels."

That said, let us acknowledge that historically there are other potential influences on climate greater than ours. The EPA website says, "For about two-thirds of the last 400 million years, geologic evidence suggests CO_2 levels and temperatures were considerably higher than present. One theory is that volcanic eruptions from rapid sea floor spreading elevated CO_2 concentrations, enhancing the greenhouse effect and raising temperatures."

Other factors to consider are variables in the earth's orbit and the sun's intensity. The sun is presently experiencing a "solar minimum" during which there is no sunspot activity. These are typically eleven-year cycles, but scientists are watching what could be an extended lull. According to NASA's website, "careful measurements by several NASA spacecraft show that the sun's brightness has dropped by 0.02% at visible wavelengths and 6% at extreme UV wavelengths since the solar minimum of 1996.

The changes so far are not enough to reverse the course of global warming, but there are some other significant side-effects: Earth's upper atmosphere is heated less by the sun."

What NASA has not mentioned is that the last significant absence of sunspot activity, called the Maunder Solar Minimum, happened between 1645 and 1715, and caused the Little Ice Age. Scientists predict regular sunspot activity will resume its cycle in 2012, but if it doesn't, we just may see a reversal of the melting of the ice caps. Wouldn't it be ironic if, in the near future, greenhouse gases were encouraged?

All things considered, the evidence is overwhelming that mankind's actions have had a great effect on climate change and that we need to act quickly. When you look at the corresponding rise of greenhouse gases and global temperatures, it's hard to argue. You certainly can't deny that our ice caps are melting.

In fact, the climate data compiled by NASA's Goddard Institute and the National Oceanic and Atmospheric Administration (NOAA) closely matches that of Great Britain's University of East Anglia's Climate Research Unit (CRU), the very one under fire after more than a thousand e-mails were hacked on the eve of the Copenhagen summit. Critics said the e-mails exposed manipulation of the data. I think that the fact that the CRU data almost mirrors the other research speaks for itself.

A *Washington Post* story in 2007 quoted Brenda Ekwurzel, a climate scientist with the Union of Concerned Scientists, a public interest group: "When you look at temperatures across the globe, every single year since 1993 has been in the top 20 warmest years on record."

The fact that the U.S. military is making contingency plans for climate change should speak volumes about the credibility of the science. At home, efforts to protect naval bases against an expected rise in water levels are under way. Military strategists are also trying to project potential hot spots that might lead to military intervention. Consider the risk. According to the Population Reference Bureau (2003), "approximately 3 billion people—about half of the world's population—live within 200 kilometers (124 miles) of a coastline. By 2025 that figure is likely to double."

What if tens of millions were suddenly displaced with no food and no shelter? Society breaks down dramatically at a time like that. It will be just as the conservatives like it—every man for himself.

If dramatically reducing our CO_2 emissions will make the difference between a stable climate or one more hostile to our existence—and the majority of scientists not on the oil lobby's payroll believe that is the case—it would be silly to have history record for our sweaty, mutant great-grandchildren that this generation wasn't willing to make the hard choices because "it might hurt the economy."

SOLUTIONS

If mankind has inadvertently influenced the climate, what's to stop us from purposely doing so in a positive way? In a recent study, the Copenhagen Consensus Center—a respected European think tank, once skeptical about climate change—concluded that 1,900 ships could create clouds by spraying seawater into the air, thereby reflecting enough of the sun's rays to thwart global warming. The cost? Three hundred million dollars per ship—a pittance when measured against the rewards. (What we don't know is how the "cloud ships" might alter rainfall and drought conditions in the world.)

No one program will save the world from climate change but Cash for Clunkers, a program that got old polluting gas guzzlers off the road, was an imaginative and successful approach. Not only did it stimulate the car industry when it was on the ropes, but it got polluters off the road. It's one small piece of the puzzle in Obama's commitment to reduce U.S. carbon emissions by 80 percent before 2050.

Another proposal to manage greenhouse gases is Cap and Trade. The program caps emissions that each country is allowed to emit. The way it would work is a government would distribute emissions credits to individual companies, some of which will be able to keep their emissions below their cap, thereby giving them the freedom to sell these "pollution permits" to others. The incentive to cut pollution is then obvious.

According to industry expert Kari Manlove, the pollution permits could be given away or auctioned off "with the funds going to alleviate rising energy prices for low- and middle-income Americans, and invest in the infrastructure and low-carbon technologies that are needed to transition our economy to one that's low carbon."

Make no mistake. This will require sacrifice. That we will sacrifice is a given. If we cannot minimize climate change, we will pay dearly. The question is, Do we have the character to sacrifice now? Perhaps that sacrifice is being forced upon us. According to the *Washington Post,* U.S. carbon emissions fell by 2.8 percent in 2008 because of the recession, the largest decline since 1982.

The ultimate test, when it comes to climate change, is the ability and willingness of industrial and emerging powers to agree on solutions. The outcome rests largely in the hands of two nations, the United States and China.

China, the world's biggest polluter, is on track to emit more carbon in the next thirty years than the United States has in our entire history. But before we get too smug, we should remember our per-capita emissions are still four times higher than China's.

No doubt it will seem disingenuous of America, as the largest energy consumer, to say, "Sure we got to build our country without all those pesky carbon caps, but the rules have changed. Do as we say, not as we did."

But the rules *have* changed, and the climate is threatening to change our world in a big way. It is imperative that we understand this threat to mankind. Even if the United States can cut carbon emissions by 80 percent before 2050, and other nations follow suit, we may not be able to avoid *significant* climate change. Maybe all we can do is avoid *catastrophic* change. We have an obligation to our children and grandchildren to try.

The stakes couldn't be higher.

CHAPTER FIVE

CONTROLLING AMERICA'S BORDERS

From Melting Pot to Meltdown

A MILLION SOLDIERS ONCE MANNED THE FOUR-THOUSAND-MILE-long Great Wall of China in an effort to keep out Nomadic tribes. It's an ominous historical reminder of the importance and difficulty of protecting national borders. Difficult? Some say futile. Even then.

Now, "You live in the age of interdependence," Bill Clinton says. "Borders don't count for much or stop much, good or bad, anymore." Yet here we are at a crossroads when it comes to illegal immigration and homeland security. Do we abandon any hope of controlling our borders, or do we cling to our sovereignty? From a utopian point of view, borders should be unnecessary, kingdoms should be dispensed with, and the goodness of man should triumph. Yet mankind has not evolved to that point. We would be fools to keep the front door unlocked.

There are two major problems with porous U.S. borders: First, we want to defend our borders against attack. Second, because the resources of any country are finite, we need to defend our economic infrastructure.

Allowing millions of illegal immigrants to live here—in the shadows—undermines the structure of our society. This shadow workforce both exploits and is exploited by our system. Its presence drives down or stagnates the wages of American workers while giving some businesses an unfair advantage over those who choose not to hire undocumented workers. It is not unusual for members of this shadow workforce to be mistreated and cheated—after all, what illegal worker is going to go to the authorities?

Any organization, whether it's the Boy Scouts or the U.S. government, needs to be able to identify its membership. The primary reason for existence of the government is to pool resources so we can collectively do what we cannot achieve individually. You have to know where the people are so you can properly allocate resources. But when it comes to illegal aliens, we don't know as much as we should.

Estimates of the number of illegal immigrants living in America range from 7 million to a 2005 Bear Stearns estimate of 20 million. The U.S. Border Patrol estimates this population to be somewhere between 12 and 15 million. The common estimate is 12 million, but we really won't know until the day we either deport all of these people (impossible) or grant them the right of citizenship, which would be a tall order.

According to Pew Hispanic Center research, "Mexico is by far the leading country of origin for U.S. immigrants, accounting for a third (32%) of all foreign-born residents and two-thirds (66%) of Hispanic immigrants."

Immigration has been put on the back burner by the Obama administration while it wrestles with other issues, like the collapsing economy and health care. Immigration reform is not an issue that will produce any kind of political capital and could well prove to be divisive enough to undermine the presidency. It would be unwise, however, for the administration to ignore the issue of illegal immigration for too long. There's an old adage that says when you find yourself in a hole, the first thing you have to do is stop digging. As long as we ignore the immigration issue, we will continue digging ourselves a deeper hole.

MANY ARE HERE TO STAY

When all the political commotion about migratory labor has come and gone, one fact will remain. You aren't going to round up 12 million Mexicans and bus them back over the border. Hell, George Bush couldn't clear out New Orleans before Hurricane Katrina, and those people *wanted* a ride! We'd have to become a police state to deport so many people.

Pragmatically, the United States could so harshly penalize people and businesses who employ illegal workers that most would be unwilling to take the risk of hiring them. Jobs would dry up. Word would go out across our borders. Immigration would slow. No administration has mustered the will to do that, but at some point we are going to have to enforce the law. The Bush administration was content to look the other way. Driving the cheap labor out of the country would upset business interests and it could harm some industries, among them agriculture, which has historically leaned on migrant workers for backbreaking labor in the fields, dairies, and apiaries. The Obama administration has to decide if it has the will and the manpower to do what previous administrations would not. Even if producers can hire enough domestic workers, these workers will not work as cheaply, and that will drive up some food prices. Certain liberals will be angry, too, because of their sensitivity to anything that could be construed as racism.

Intellectually, we know that the inability to control our borders is bad for the economy and bad for our country in general, and cannot continue. But what about the illegal workers that are already here? This is a hot potato that neither party will take on alone—nor should they. If ever the two parties needed each other for political cover, this is the issue. If we, as a nation, can muster the political will to strictly enforce labor laws and penalize employers who hire undocumented workers, many undocumented workers will return home.

Then—and here's where Big Eddie's reality check comes in—after the dust has settled, what you have to do is create a process to allow those remaining—with the exception of those with criminal records—U.S. citizenship. Failure to do so means relegating these undocumented workers to a no-man's-land where they can be forced to work for next to nothing and live in poverty, essentially forming a permanent underclass.

I predict the Republicans will fight any reasonable plan tooth and nail for a number of reasons. For one thing, they are the party of big business, and big business loves the way cheap labor suppresses wages and kills unions. Their natural instinct is to do what is right for the pocketbooks of industry rather than what is best for the American worker and the country as a whole, long-term.

Second, Republicans are scared to death that most of those Mexican-Americans, if ever granted citizenship, will vote for Democrats and sink the GOP for generations. Third, there is a racist streak a mile wide running through the Republican Party. It may come in the form of code words and innuendo, but it is there just the same. There is real fear of diversity. According to Pew Research, by 2050, Hispanics will make up 29 percent of the population in the United States.

At this point in our immigration discussion, it is important to offer some perspective and remember that many people of Mexican heritage are indigenous to the Southwest. Since the signing of the Treaty of Guadalupe Hidalgo in 1848, which expanded U.S. territory, generations of Mexicans have been living in and providing migratory labor in places like California, Nevada, Utah, Arizona, New Mexico, Colorado, and Wyoming. In other words, their presence here is completely natural.

We all know America has been strengthened through legal immigration. From Einstein to Edward Teller to Isaac Stern to Cesar Chavez, immigrants have transformed our country. But unchecked, illegal immigration threatens to overwhelm our resources. With high unemployment, we simply have to look out for the American worker—and that includes the Hispanic Americans who are here legally.

ILLEGAL IMMIGRANT IMPACT

It's no surprise that so many people want to come to America. It is still a country that blesses its citizens with limitless ways to better their lot in life. And despite the very real class warfare going on here against the American worker and the middle class, the United States remains a land of opportunity and hope. If you weren't here, you'd want to be.

Who can fault a young Mexican for slipping across the border for a job that will save his family from poverty? NAFTA (the North American Free Trade Agreement) was supposed to change all that, and indeed, many American factories (and jobs) did relocate to Mexico. But then many of those factories and jobs moved on to China and India, where an even cheaper labor force undercuts even the wages of the poorly paid Mexicans, in a global race to the bottom line. This is a race that only the top brass at international corporations can win.

If we cannot slow illegal immigration to a trickle, the whole notion of granting citizenship to those already here is pointless. With one hand we should welcome these new citizens. With the other, we have to shut the door behind them.

Conservatives like to say there are some jobs Americans won't do, but I don't believe that. If you are an American carpenter with a mortgage, health care premiums, and kids in college, you cannot afford to work as cheaply as an undocumented Mexican carpenter.

The combination of low-cost labor from Mexico and outsourcing to low-cost laborers in China and India has conspired to stagnate or shrink the wages of the average American worker. By playing one workforce against another in countries that don't have the restrictions against pollution we do, corporations profit handsomely while minimizing any advancement of the human condition.

Global economics are incredibly complex, but it is very clear to me that America has the most to lose and that in America today, the biggest loser of all is the middle class, the very economic engine that built this nation. Jobs go to China through the front door; cheap labor streams across the border through the back door—all to the advantage of big business. Jobs go to the lowest bidder.

Even if you ignore the fact that illegal workers depress American wages and disposable income, there is an argument that each low-skilled illegal immigrant is a net drain on our society. Robert Rector, a scholar at the conservative Heritage Foundation, said in his study *The Fiscal Cost of Low-Skill Households to the U.S. Taxpayer* that two thirds of illegal immigrants fall under the "low skill" category. Using government figures, he calculated wages, taxes paid, and how much aid low-skill workers receive from government programs. He asserted that the average low-skill household received $22,449 *more* in benefits each year than it paid in taxes.

Take education for instance. In California, the sixth largest economy in the world, where 7 percent of the population (2.7 million) is illegal, according to the Pew Hispanic Center, the annual cost of educating a student in public school is well over $7,000. In 2009, with state government groaning under a $27 billion deficit, some citizens advocated denying welfare benefits to the illegal immigrant parents of U.S.-born children, something proponents say would save $640 billion a year. Overall, California officials, as reported by the *Los Angeles Times,* estimate the cost of illegal immigrants to the state in education, jails, roads, police, and fire protection to be as high as $6 billion a year.

Yes, these illegal workers do contribute to the economy. The Social Security Administration reported a net gain of $12 billion in 2007 from undocumented workers.

We can look at these numbers until we're blue in the face, but the big picture is still this: There are 12 million people illegally in the United States at a time (November 2009) when there are more than 15 million Americans looking for a job.

This is about jobs.

Senator Byron Dorgan (D-ND) says there is no social program as effective as a good job. This isn't a case of the handouts and entitlements the conservatives complain about; this is about getting Americans back to work. Conservatives shouldn't continue to support, under the table, cheap illegal labor and then complain about the cost of safety nets for unemployed Americans. Of course, most conservatives haven't connected the dots.

Isn't it obvious that this is an issue we have to face before it gets any worse? If it is not a crisis now, it is a crisis waiting to happen.

POSITIVE SIGNS

One of the best ways to stem the tide of illegal immigrants from Mexico is for the Mexican economy to bloom. Things may be trending the right way for the Mexican labor force. According to *BusinessWeek,* "in 1996, Chinese labor cost about one-third [as much as] Mexican labor. Today, Chinese labor costs are about half of Mexico's—$1.69 per hour, on average, in 2007, compared to $3.46 per hour, according to the International Labor Organization (ILO). In another year or two, according to estimates, hiring a Chinese worker will cost about 85% of what it costs to hire a Mexican worker."

If the cost of production in Mexico—and labor is always a big (often the biggest) influence on costs—becomes competitive with China, it stands to reason that more production will take place domestically in Mexico. That means more jobs for Mexicans, which should take some pressure off the border.

THE NEW NORMAL

For better or worse, there is a great economic leavening going on when it comes to the global workforce. The result is what people are starting to call the New Normal. We saw the symptoms under George W. Bush when wages stagnated and began to creep backward. Median household income, adjusted for inflation, declined from $47,599 in 2000 to $46,326 in 2005—a $1,273 average loss per family. Of course the scheme to enrich the rich at the expense of the middle class wasn't hatched under Bush II (though he did nothing to stop it), it was hatched in the Reagan years. I'm sure in twenty years die-hard unemployed conservatives will still build altars to Reagan in their tent cities across America. Some people never catch on.

While the North American Free Trade Agreement was initiated under George Herbert Walker Bush, Bill Clinton became NAFTA's champion—to my mind the biggest mistake of his presidency. That giant sucking sound you heard, as Ross Perot predicted, was an estimated 1.7 million jobs lost to NAFTA from 1994 to 2002. Industries in California, New York, Michigan, and Texas were hit especially hard.

NAFTA was supposed to be a miracle cure for our illegal immigration woes. Instead, with Chinese workers working for less than Mexicans, Mexico found itself losing jobs to China. By 2003, according to the *Voice of America,* 170 Mexican factories had relocated to China.

George W. Bush followed up Clinton's NAFTA mistake with pure indifference to the increased pressures on American families. His lack of oversight encouraged health care premiums to skyrocket 80 percent on his watch. Energy costs climbed dramatically, too. Gas was $1.47 when Bush took office; it hit $4.00 on his watch. And the cost of a college education rose 44 percent during Dubya's years at the helm. It is pretty obvious that he was much more concerned with taking care of big business than with watching out for the average American.

While middle-class Americans were taking it on the chin, gross domestic product was on the rise. Big business was making a killing at the expense of the labor force. As the *Wall Street Journal* put it in 2006, "Since the end of the recession of 2001, a lot of the growth in GDP per person— that is, productivity—has gone to profits, not wages." And for many workers, there soon were not many wages at all.

From the start of the recession in 2007 to October 2009, the economy shed 7.2 million jobs, according to the Associated Press. While 3.4 million of those jobs were lost under Obama's administration, it would be unfair to hang that on him. He walked into Bush's economic buzz saw.

"This Great Recession is an inflection point for the economy in many respects. I think the unemployment rate will be permanently higher, or at least higher for the foreseeable future," said Mark Zandi, chief economist and cofounder of Moody's Economy.com, on October 19, 2009, according to AP. "Many factors are pushing against a quick recovery," added Heidi Shierholz, an economist at the labor-oriented Economic Policy Institute, in that same report. "Things will come back. But it's going to take a long time. I think we will likely see elevated unemployment at least until 2014."

If things continue to progress as they have, the New Normal may well mean that our children will enjoy a lower standard of living than their parents. In places like China and India, meanwhile, the quality of life will improve steadily.

MEXICO—A FAILED STATE?

Despite a few encouraging economic signs, Mexico's future is far from certain. A brutal drug war raging along our border could undermine everything both governments are working on.

Remarkably, the U.S. Joint Forces Command said in 2009 that the two countries most at risk of becoming failed states were Pakistan and *Mexico*. Why didn't that astonishing statement make national headlines? Bill Clinton's drug czar, General Barry McCaffrey, said, "The dangerous and worsening problems in Mexico . . . fundamentally threaten U.S. national security." Should Mexico come apart at the seams, America could become one giant refugee camp.

Almost thirteen thousand people have been killed in Mexico's drug war since 2006. Murder, kidnapping, and other violent crimes have leaked into American cities along the Mexican border. If the American media has not paid much attention to this threat, our government has.

By mid-2009, less than three years after Bush authorized it, the United States had built almost all of the planned seven hundred miles of fence in hot-spot areas along the shared two-thousand-mile U.S.–Mexico border. Meanwhile, the Obama administration has doubled border enforcement security teams and beefed up the border presence of Drug Enforcement (DEA) and Bureau of Alcohol, Tobacco, Firearms and Explosives (ATF) agents.

And that border patrol faces a formidable enemy. The Associated Press says there are six main drug cartels and twenty-four drug lords causing most of the carnage. These are brutal, brutal people. According to a March 2009 report from the *Economist,* "just before Christmas the severed heads of eight Mexican soldiers were found dumped in plastic bags near a shopping centre in Chilpancingo. . . . Another three were found in an icebox near the border city of Ciudad Juárez. Farther along the border near Tijuana police detained Santiago Meza, nicknamed El Pozolero ('the soupmaker'), who confessed to having dissolved the bodies of more than 300 people in acid over the past nine years on the orders of a local drug baron."

Mexican president Felipe Calderón, who was elected in 2006, immediately assigned forty-five thousand army troops to fight the cartels, who are armed with rocket launchers, grenades, machine guns, and armor-piercing ammunition. In August 2009, the Mexican government implemented another dramatic change. *All* customs agents, many of them believed to be linked to contraband operations, were replaced by the Mexican Army. Calderón believes the increasingly pitched fighting since then is proof that the cartels are feeling the pressure. Other analysts don't believe the battle is even competitive.

If I were counseling President Obama on national security, I would tell him to pay careful attention to Mexico. Efforts to secure our border with barbwire and border agents can only go so far. We need to have a strategy of support for the Mexican government in its internal struggle against drug cartels.

And I think we need to look inward, because, after all, the American appetite for drugs is what perpetuates this cycle of corruption and violence. Some argue that we ought to end this prohibition against drugs. Legalize them, tax them, and deal with the addiction. I understand the argument, but I struggle with that. Either way, the American market for illegal drugs is an enormous topic, big enough for another, different book. I'll say this much now, though: It's time for a coherent national discussion about drugs.

CHAPTER SIX

THE CHINA DRAGON

The Rise of an Economic Superpower and What That Means for Us

REMEMBER WHEN YOU WERE A KID PLAYING KING OF THE HILL, HOW much easier it was to become the king than it was to stay there? Everywhere you looked, someone was coming to knock you off. After World War II, the United States found itself at the top of the hill, with the world's mightiest economic and military machine, in large part because all the other economic machines in Europe had been devastated.

While by all measures today the United States has the mightiest military, many experts believe we will soon be knocked off as economic King of the Hill by China. And since you can only field the army you can afford, it's not a leap to think that our status as the world's greatest military power is threatened, too.

A 2005 survey by Reuters in nine countries showed that most respondents considered *economic power* the key to national power, but in China and in the United States, most respondents believed *military* power was more crucial.

China increased defense spending by 14.9 percent in 2009—to more than $70 billion. While that was the lowest increase in three years, as the country grappled with the economic crisis and domestic issues, the buildup has the Pentagon wary.

"They are developing capabilities that are . . . maritime and air focused, and in many ways, very much focused on us," Admiral Michael Mullen said in a separate story from Reuters. "They seem very focused on the United States Navy and our bases that are in that part of the world."

China's estimated military spending equals 1.4 percent of its GDP, which is $3.5 trillion. Officially, the United States spends about 4 percent of its $13.8 trillion GDP on defense, which, in 2009, translated to about $515 billion. In the Clinton years, defense was cut from 5 percent to 3 percent of GDP, which helped reduce deficit spending.

The 2005 Reuters survey mentioned above showed that seven out of every ten Chinese citizens believes their country will be a world power by 2020. Forty-four percent believe they have already achieved that status. It's hard to argue. The Chinese, all 1.3 billion of them, are at the table and their stack of chips is growing. Goldman Sachs predicts that China's GDP could equal ours by 2027.

In his book *Hegemon: China's Plan to Dominate Asia and the World*, Steven W. Mosher talks about the mind-set of the emerging generation in China: "Their political education has veered away from ideology in favor of nationalism: they have been made familiar with the glories of China's imperial past, and with the history of her humiliation at the hands of the Western powers. They have been taught, and have come to believe, that America is denying China her rightful place in the world."

The Chinese super-power strategy is two-pronged: First, maneuver us into a massive trade imbalance, and, second, use part of their profits to build up militarily. Obtusely, American corporations that have profited by and encouraged cheap Chinese imports—hello, Walmart—have not only been selling out the American worker, but America itself, by funding the very Chinese military that we may have to face in years to come. It's no different than the way we fund Islamic extremism through oil profits because we lack the discipline to wean ourselves off imported oil.

Which of the twin prongs—economic strength or military might— will China exercise to become King of the Hill? Probably both. When China's economy is less dependent upon ours, we can expect them to test their muscle.

The obvious first test is Taiwan—the island nation that the People's Republic of China considers part of mainland China. While, at one point, President Bush indicated that the United States would defend Taiwan against a Chinese invasion, that position has seemingly softened, and wisely so. There is a big difference between rattling sabers at Tehran and rattling them at Beijing. China has eight hundred missiles aimed at Taiwan now. And they are building up their fleet to neutralize the U.S. Navy.

As groundbreaking as it was for Nixon to go to China in 1972, the most important diplomatic missions are yet to come. While there are distractions domestically as well as around the globe, diplomatic relations with the Chinese will be of utmost importance for America.

THE CHINESE CENTURY

You have to credit the Chinese for their ability to transform their economy. They may not have beaten us at their game—communism—but they sure might beat us at ours.

Many signs point to this being the Chinese Century. One of the most obvious indicators is that China holds more U.S. government debt than any other country—about $1 trillion and counting, by late 2009. The proposed U.S. budget for 2010 calls for about $3.55 trillion in spending and a $1.17 trillion deficit. So how do we cover the shortfall? Through the sale of U.S. government–backed securities that pay the holder interest.

So, China is doing us a favor by investing in us, by financing our deficit. But it's not so good for us in the long term. Essentially, as a nation, we are running up our credit card and leaving the bill to the grandkids.

As long as that credit card interest outpaces inflation, all is well and good for investors.

But increasingly factors like the potentially inflationary stimulus package have China, Japan, and the UK—the top three holders of U.S. debt—skittish. A weakening dollar stands to kill the profit on a lower interest investment like U.S. securities.

Weak currency does have its theoretical advantages, in that it makes exports cheaper (from the country with the weaker currency) and can serve to lower the trade imbalance between countries. A lower dollar means it is cheaper for other countries to purchase things that are "Made in the U.S.A." That keeps factories humming and workers working. One of my mantras in life is that in every economy there is opportunity, so even in a recession, a smart businessperson can find niche areas of growth.

Not surprisingly, the weak dollar had Republicans, including Sarah Palin, criticizing the Obama administration. She failed to note (and probably didn't know) that the dollar was even weaker under Bush in his last months in office than it was under Obama in the third quarter of 2009. *New York Times* economist Paul Krugman says, "The truth is that the falling dollar is good news. For one thing, it's mainly the result of rising confidence: the dollar rose at the height of the financial crisis as panicked investors sought safe haven in America, and it's falling again now that the fear is subsiding. And a lower dollar is good for U.S. exporters, helping us make the transition away from huge trade deficits to a more sustainable international position."

The dirty little difference between China and our other international bankers is that China "pegs" the value of its currency—the yuan—to the dollar. The tactic has been controversial in the United States because if the yuan is pegged artificially low, it exacerbates the huge trade deficit America has in relation to China—that U.S. deficit was $270 billion in 2008, according to U.S. government data.

In 2005, China had seemingly decoupled the yuan from the dollar, but when the economic crisis hit in late 2008, the yuan and the dollar were coupled again—to defend the status quo—which, again, has been large trade deficits for America. Had the yuan appreciated in value, American products would theoretically have become more attractive in China.

Federal Reserve chairman Ben Bernanke believes the trade deficit was a major cause of the global financial crisis. He warned, "Asian countries needed to rely less on exports and more on their consumption at home for their economic growth." Bernanke also advised the Chinese to create social safety nets to address the volatility of capitalism.

Hold the phone! Rewind that! Did the Fed chief just call for safety net programs in China? Isn't that like socialism or communism or some other *ism*? Holy smokes, let's hope Republicans don't read that. They'll demand to see his birth certificate or NRA card or something. Republicans have always stood against such safety nets, viewing poverty and even unemployment as some self-inflicted disease.

Late in 2009, when the Democrats sought to expand unemployment benefits by twenty weeks, Republicans stalled the legislation—anything to obstruct the Obama agenda. Senator Dick Durbin (D-IL) scolded them: "They want to drag it out. They have no sensitivity to these people who lost their job or are struggling to keep their families together under the most difficult circumstances."

I don't get it. Republican policies helped break Humpty Dumpty, but now they don't want to help put him back together again. The Republicans seem to view the unemployed as collateral damage in their effort to politically damage the president.

CHINA'S BOLD REACTION TO THE ECONOMIC CRISIS

Now that China has adopted Western-style capitalism and all of its trappings, its people have much different expectations than their parents and grandparents had. This generation of Chinese is growing accustomed to a higher standard of living. Any sudden negative shock to the Chinese economy has the potential to cause a great deal of social unrest. The Chinese authoritarian government can ill afford unrest, so in reaction to the global recession, they aggressively pumped $1 trillion in stimulus money into their economy.

It worked. The *Economic Times* reported in October 2009, "The Chinese economy expanded at a rapid rate of 8.9 per cent in the third quarter of 2009 as compared to the year-ago period, mainly boosted by increased infrastructure investment and stimulus measures. The world's fastest growing economy, which has been less affected by the global financial meltdown, grew 7.9 per cent in the June quarter." According to the Chinese government, China's GDP was up 6.1 percent for the first quarter, 7.9 percent for the second, and 8.9 percent for the third quarter of 2009.

Why was China able to bounce back so quickly? Because of the fiscal discipline the Chinese showed when things were good. The Chinese inherited a budget surplus just like the one Bush inherited from Bill Clinton, but the Chinese used their budget surpluses to invest in infrastructure and job creation. What did Bush do? He spilled so much red ink it looked like a horror movie—*Night of the Living Dumbasses*. By failing to address the trade deficit and by squandering so much money, the Bush administration, for all its tough talk and saber rattling, weakened the country.

In September 2008, in the early stages of the global financial meltdown, Japan sold off $13 billion of U.S. debt while China boldly took on $44 billion in new debt. The net effect is that purchase of U.S. securities tends to strengthen the dollar, which, of course, allows the favorable trade situation for China to continue.

In a very telling remark confirming this strategy, Lueo Ping of the China Regulatory Commission, speaking at the Global Association of Risk Professionals' Risk Management Convention in February 2009, said: "Except for U.S. Treasuries, what can you hold? Gold? You don't hold Japanese government bonds or UK bonds. U.S. Treasuries are the safe haven. For everyone, including China, it is the only option. We hate you guys. Once you start issuing $1 trillion to $2 trillion . . . we know the dollar is going to depreciate, so we hate you guys but there is nothing much we can do."

CODEPENDENT COUNTRIES

It's an interesting dynamic. Ironically, if China is to become the number one economic power, they need our marketplace to get there. For now, that gives us some leverage in this odd economic partnership. And for the time being we have to dance together.

Strategically, from China's point of view, to take the next step to global preeminence, they need to be able to extricate themselves somewhat from this economic entanglement with the United States and find or develop equally rewarding investments and trading partners elsewhere.

And that is already happening. According to the *Globalist,* an online magazine focused on the global economy, "few people outside China and India are aware that by the end of 2007, China had become India's number one trading partner. From China's side, India is now one of its top ten trading partners." China is also promoting a European Union–style trade bloc among Asian nations, as part of the plan to lessen its dependence on the American consumer. A free trade pact between China and the ten-member Association of Southeast Asian Nations has already been signed.

Also, as its population becomes more affluent and begins to consume more domestic goods, China will not need to rely as much on the U.S. market.

As our rival—and make no mistake, that's how they see us—the Chinese want to knock us off the hill, but at the moment we are so codependent we would drag them down with us. Like us, they need a level of independence and self-sufficiency. And for that, we just have to go back to my Four Pillars. Like any great nation, China needs to feed, defend, and educate its people as well as have a sound fiscal policy. Feeding the country is no problem. Their Achilles' heel, like ours, is a ravenous thirst for oil.

With a rapidly expanding manufacturing base and the growing affluence of its society, China's hunger for energy continues to grow. Most of the oil guzzled in America goes into automobiles. Now, the Chinese, too, have fallen in love with the car. China's total motor vehicle number will increase from 80 million to 220 million by 2020; this can only exacerbate supply and price concerns.

Our country went to war with Iraq to secure the petroleum necessary for our defense. If we did it, do you think Communist China would have any compunction about doing the same? The *Los Angeles Times* reports that China continues to aggressively secure oil leases around the world, including in the Gulf of Mexico, the source of one fourth of America's domestic production. The story notes, "The sour U.S. economy and the need for Washington and Beijing to cooperate on potentially larger issues could mute any outcry. The U.S. could also find it difficult to rebuff China when it has long welcomed other foreign investment in the gulf. . . . The U.S. risks undercutting its foreign policy goals as well. Concern is growing over China's aggressive investment in oil-rich nations with anti-U.S. regimes, including Iran and Sudan. Denying China a shot at drilling in U.S. waters would only encourage Beijing to make deals in volatile regions given that new oil reserves in stable, democratic nations are getting harder to find."

When you consider China's aggressive pursuit of oil reserves, it suggests that there is potential trouble ahead between our nations unless both countries can make the switch from fossil fuels to green energy quickly. Globally, can we produce enough green energy to decrease the demand for oil? The answer to that question will have much to say about whether the coming decades will be peaceful or full of conflict.

This situation is frustrating to me and harkens back to what I said in the early pages of this book. As a nation, we have to "fly ahead of the airplane." We have to have a long-range domestic and global strategy. Jimmy Carter called for energy independence in the 1970s, but today, we are more dependent for oil than ever on repressive countries that we have enriched and empowered. And they like our dollars more than they like us. Meanwhile, from a strategic standpoint, China is doing all the right things.

Fareed Zakaria, *Newsweek* columnist and one of the most astute observers of global politics, wrote, "China is also well aware of its dependence on imported oil and is acting in surprisingly farsighted ways. It now spends more on solar, wind, and battery technology than the United States does. Research by the investment bank Lazard Freres shows that of the top 10 companies (by market capitalization) in these three fields, four are Chinese. (Only three are American.) It is also making a massive investment in higher education."

As Americans, we have to come to grips with the weakness of our political system when it comes to long-range planning. The parties in charge must find common ground and common goals that we can pursue without interruption by the election cycle. This is what China has done, and China is gaining ground fast. The Chinese will prevail unless we can unite as a country.

I believe that we have the right guy at the helm right now, but we have an opposition party more invested in his failure than in America's success. The divide in our country today is every bit as serious as it was in the Civil War. We are not shooting at one another, but we are bringing ourselves down just the same. As a voter, you have a huge responsibility to put into office people who can revive the art of compromise. United we stand. Divided we fall.

This is not about nationalism. I just know in my heart that in order for this to be a better world in which people can live in a dignified manner, America must succeed. We are still the world's last best hope. In spite of the many flaws in our system, at the heart of it is the Constitution, a road map for a better world.

CHAPTER SEVEN

CLEANING UP
AFTER BUSH II

How Reckless Fiscal and Foreign Policies
Almost Sank Us

I SAT UP ASTONISHED WHEN I HEARD THE NEWS THAT BARACK OBAMA
had won the Nobel Peace Prize. As Bill Maher put it, "How hard can it
be to get a black professor and a white cop to sit down for a beer?" Kidding aside, it appeared to me that the president won the award less than
a year after his election for the transformational effect he has had in
America and around the world.

Set aside the bitter conservative negativity for a moment, and you
can see what history will choose as a defining moment for this country.
Not only did we elect an African-American, but the election was also a
repudiation of George W. Bush, Dick Cheney, and the insidious effect
they were having on our country and the world. I felt like the Dixie
Chicks—eventually, I grew ashamed of my president. I don't ever want
to go there again. Even though I have been angry, disappointed, and
frustrated with Barack Obama during his first year in office, I cannot
imagine a time when I will ever be ashamed of him.

The Nobel Peace Prize was also a repudiation of the dangerous
negativity of the conservative right in America. Naturally, they sneered
when the American president was announced as the winner.

On *Saturday Night Live,* Seth Meyers reported, "Republican Committee chairman Michael Steele [a black man] criticized President Obama's Nobel Peace Prize win, asking, 'What has President Obama actually accomplished?' Well, for starters, Michael Steele, if it weren't for Obama, you wouldn't have *your* job."

The Republicans have all the political subtlety of a musk ox. This is the party that produced Karl Rove, who used a smear campaign in the South to suggest that John McCain's adopted black daughter was an illegitimate love child. Mississippi governor Haley Barbour proudly supports the state flag, which incorporates the Confederate banner. South Carolina continues to fly the Confederate flag on its capitol grounds. And Nixon's divisive "Southern Strategy," and its veiled racism, remains alive and well.

Six months into his administration, anyone could see that the tactic of the Republicans, bereft of any real solutions to the nation's ills, was to try to discredit Obama at every turn, whether it was justified or not. Politically, they acted like ill-tempered teenagers throwing a tantrum. By this point, they are in danger of losing any remaining credibility.

Senator James Inhofe, the Republican from Oklahoma, said, "This [Nobel Prize] just reemphasizes how this president has moved the United States from a foreign policy of strong national defense to one based on multinational cooperation. That is the kind of change that the Nobel committee believes in."

Though he meant it as an insult, Inhofe was only partly wrong. One of the most important things the president did in his first year was to reach out to countries snubbed by the previous administration. What Inhofe got wrong was the suggestion that Obama is looking to weaken national defense. To the contrary, by showing a willingness to cooperate and employ diplomacy, Obama did something historic. He used common sense instead of saber rattling. But you can see how the whole concept of cooperation might confuse a Republican like Inhofe.

Global politics are a lot like golf. You have to use the right club for the right situation. The Bush administration's response to every situation was to pull out the driver—even in the sand traps. Obama has shown a willingness to use a pitching wedge and a putter. By shelving a defensive missile shield in eastern Europe, something Russia viewed as provocative, Obama and America sent a message that we are serious about peace and nuclear arms reduction. With so many pots boiling over—so many crises—the implications of such visionary actions will not be broadly understood for years, but I believe that Obama is trying to take the essential steps now to minimize the chance for catastrophic global conflicts in the future. He understands that the days of the United States being able to dominate as the big kid on the block are gone. America may have a superior military, but global cooperation is the best weapon against rogue states and terrorists.

With the global financial crisis at full boil when he took office, it was easy to lose sight of the larger global mess Barack Obama inherited. George Bush left two unfinished wars behind. Despicably, his administration perpetrated a sales job for the Iraq War that was predicated on bad intelligence and deceit. There were no weapons of mass destruction. There were no chemical weapons. There was no yellowcake uranium from Niger. Despite the fact that most Americans supported a war on al-Qaeda's network in Afghanistan, the administration pushed the issue along with what turned out to be a false premise.

In his State of the Union address on January 29, 2002, less than six months after the attacks on the World Trade Center and the Pentagon, Bush told a jittery nation, "We have found diagrams of American nuclear power plants and public water facilities" in caves used by al-Qaeda. Two years later, the Bush administration admitted that no such diagrams had been found. But by then, they had support not only for the Afghanistan War but to go into Iraq as well, presumably as a reaction to terrorism. Of course we know now that the neocons were looking for a "New Pearl Harbor" to get the public behind a war and what was viewed as unfinished business in Iraq. This was no secret. The right wing think tank Project for the New American Century published a treatise on the subject prior to 2000. Ten members of the think tank were involved in the Bush II administration, including Dick Cheney, former secretary of defense Donald Rumsfeld, and his deputy, Paul Wolfowitz.

It's interesting to see how the fall of the Berlin Wall and the triumph of democracy over communism forced a rethinking of global strategy. Suddenly, America was the world's lone superpower. In 1992, Wolfowitz, along with Cheney's former chief of staff (and later convicted felon) Scooter Libby, wrote a new mission statement, which was later rewritten by Dick Cheney himself. The original draft was leaked to the press and may still be found on the PBS website.

It said, "Our first objective is to prevent the re-emergence of a new rival. [This] *requires that we endeavor to prevent any hostile power from dominating a region whose resources would, under consolidated control, be sufficient to generate global power.*" The policy outlined other security concerns: "*access to vital raw materials, primarily Persian Gulf oil,* proliferation of weapons of mass destruction and ballistic missiles, threats to U.S. citizens from terrorism or regional or local conflict, and threats to U.S. society from narcotics trafficking" (emphasis mine).

If necessary, the United States should not be shy about taking unilateral action, the document said, adding that what is most important is "the sense that the world order is ultimately backed by the U.S." and that "the United States should be postured to act independently when collective action cannot be orchestrated" or in a crisis that calls for quick response. That is the plan the Bush-Cheney White House followed right into Iraq and Afghanistan.

The cavalier attitude with which Bush and Cheney went to war in Iraq was both criminal and vacant of morality. As a nation, we have lost sight of what war really is all about. It is too easy to become numb or oblivious to the heartbreak of war, and that isn't good.

I found it deplorable that when President Obama greeted the re-
turning bodies of eighteen troops killed in Afghanistan, Liz Cheney
suggested it was for publicity. When her father, Dick Cheney, and President Bush had done the same thing, she said, there had never been
cameras—except neither Bush nor Cheney *ever* honored fallen American
soldiers by meeting the plane and watching the unloading of the caskets
as Obama did while he was contemplating sending more troops to Afghanistan. President Obama did an honorable thing—what every commander in chief should do: look the families of the fallen in the eye.

Equally as deplorable as Liz Cheney's comments were those of Big
Daddy Dick Cheney, rising from a crypt in an undisclosed location to
accuse the president of "dithering" on the issue of troop increases. My
colleague the great Chris Matthews opined on MSNBC's *Hardball* that
perhaps Cheney should have "dithered" before sending troops into Iraq
in an unprovoked war that placed American troops in the middle of a
civil war. For the record, those weren't rose petals in the streets, Mr.
Cheney. They were pools of blood.

WHAT ABOUT AFGHANISTAN?

The tragedy of Afghanistan is that after routing the Taliban and driving
out al-Qaeda, Bush too quickly turned his focus to Iraq—the real
prize—and began pulling assets from Afghanistan for the buildup to
the Iraq War. So by the time Obama took office, the Taliban had reas-
serted itself, and America was faced with the prospect of essentially "re-
winning" the Afghanistan War, which forced President Obama to add
another 35,000 troops to the 68,000 already there. NATO also added
7,000 troops to their 39,000 troops already in Afghanistan.

But increasing troop levels is a treacherous gambit, too. It's hard not
to see the war becoming a bloody sinkhole like Vietnam. American casualties, more than eight hundred in November of 2009, continued to
mount under a resurgent enemy.

They call Afghanistan the place where empires go to die. The Soviet Union crumbled after ten years there. The last successful invaders were the Mongols in 1221, so unless you've got Genghis Khan suiting up, it could be rough going. The United States has been in Afghanistan since 2001. Bush failed because he didn't have the courage to ask the American people for the overwhelming force needed not only to win but *hold and stabilize* the country. Instead, he moved on to Iraq, leaving Afghanistan to fester like an open wound.

A report of the Senate Committee on Foreign Relations in 2009 said, "The failure to finish the job represents a lost opportunity that forever altered the course of the conflict in Afghanistan and the future of international terrorism, leaving the American people more vulnerable to terrorism, laying the foundation for today's protracted Afghan insurgency and inflaming the internal strife now endangering Pakistan."

The report goes further, damning Secretary of Defense Donald Rumsfeld and the Bush administration for not sending in the snipers, special forces, and other soldiers to finish off that bastard bin Laden when we had him cornered. This was more than a mistake in my mind. It was incompetence. While bin Laden, convinced he was about to die, prayed, Bush, Cheney, and Rumsfeld dithered.

The report reads, "Fewer than 100 American commandos were on the scene with their Afghan allies and calls for reinforcements to launch an assault were rejected. Requests were also turned down for U.S. troops to block the mountain paths leading to sanctuary a few miles away in Pakistan. The vast array of American military power, from sniper teams to the most mobile divisions of the Marine Corps and the Army, was kept on the sidelines."

While we're at it, let's discuss the "yeah but" response I can already hear from Republicans that Bill Clinton had his opportunities to take out bin Laden, too. As a matter of record, cruise missiles were fired into Afghanistan in 1998 to get bin Laden, but it turned out he wasn't there. This was in response the bombing of U.S. African embassies in Dar es

Salaam and Nairobi earlier in 1998 that killed more than two hundred, including twelve Americans. The Canadian Broadcasting Corporation reports that after the failed missile strike, Clinton ordered the CIA to try to capture bin Laden. Later in 1998, Clinton decided against another cruise missile attack on Kandahar, Afghanistan, because bin Laden was located near a mosque and it was feared the mosque might be struck and as many as two hundred civilians killed. Clinton's last opportunity came in 1999, during his final days as president, when bin Laden was falcon hunting in Afghanistan. A strike was called off because bin Laden was with senior officials of the United Arab Emirates, among America's closest allies in the Persian Gulf. Clinton had to decide whether or not to take out bin Laden and almost certainly kill the UAE officials, and then leave the fallout to the incoming president, George W. Bush.

That was the rationale. Bill Clinton told Bush that not getting bin Laden was his biggest regret, and he warned Bush that al-Qaeda would be a top priority, a warning we know Bush ignored. Now President Obama is charged with cleaning up the mess.

The long-range Obama plan is to train an Afghan army of 134,000 and a police force of 82,000 by 2011, but other strategic estimates suggest that a force of 325,000 will be needed. It's a tall order. It has taken six years to produce 250,000 soldiers in Iraq.

Americans, fueled by the trauma of the 9/11 attacks, largely felt that this was a justified war, but in retrospect, I can't help but believe that had Al Gore been president on 9/11, our response would have been more measured and more successful. And I think he would have stopped reading *The Pet Goat* after the first plane hit the World Trade Center. Bush got into a war without any plan for an end game, and then he compounded his mistake by diverting American resources from Afghanistan r the war in Iraq, essentially snatching defeat from the jaws of victory.

Before we go any further, we have to define what we can call success 'hanistan. Are we nation building? Certainly we will be well served by helping rebuild infrastructure in Afghanistan, which we quite famously failed to do after covertly supporting the Afghan effort to drive the Soviets out in 1989. Historians will always contemplate whether a small investment in schools and other infrastructure might have kept the ravaged country from becoming a breeding ground for terrorism. We missed an opportunity to create an ally in a strategic part of the world.

So, at this point, how do you stabilize the country in light of the divisions within it? There was a civil war going on before we invaded. On one side you have the U.S.-backed Northern Alliance militia, which is recognized by the United Nations as the Afghan government, aligned with the Karzai government in Kabul, and on the other the tenacious and religiously repressive Taliban, the former government that just won't stay defeated.

Our support of the Karzai government is troublesome, especially in light of widespread election fraud in 2009 and other corruption. Certainly, his approach to social issues does not seem far removed from that of the Taliban. For instance, in 2009, Karzai approved of a new law that allows a husband to starve his wife if she refuses his sexual demands. Meanwhile, I believe the Taliban is every bit as committed to winning as the North Vietnamese were. You have to understand. They view us as invaders, despite the fact that we played a large part in the defeat of the Soviet Union in Afghanistan. That was more than two decades ago.

Perhaps success can best be measured by making sure the country is forever free of al-Qaeda. Many members of the Taliban regret the association with the terrorists, especially in light of the war it provoked. A Taliban statement in October 2009 said, "We did not have any agenda to harm other countries, including Europe, nor do we have such an agenda today. Still, if you want to turn the country of the proud and pious Afghans into a colony, then know that we have an unwavering determination and have braced for a prolonged war."

The easy answer is to negotiate an agreement with the Taliban that they keep al-Qaeda out. But even if we can negotiate with the Taliban, what about their enemies and *our* allies, the Northern Alliance and the Karzai government? The rap on America is that we are not to be trusted. We come in, we prop up a government, and then we abandon it. It happened in South Vietnam, and it certainly happened when we abandoned the mujahideen (holy warriors) in Afghanistan after the defeat of the USSR.

In a perfect world we would broker a truce between the factions and create a stable environment in which credible elections could eventually be held. Perhaps stabilizing the country is the best we can do. But once the country has been stabilized, the United States ought to lead an international effort to rebuild it, starting with hospitals and schools and other infrastructure.

Increasing troop levels in Afghanistan is a tricky and expensive business. A rough White House formula places the cost of a soldier in Afghanistan at $1 million a year. Afghanistan is landlocked, four hundred miles from any port, making it very difficult to supply. Because the Taliban has been able to destroy convoys with such success, 30 to 40 percent of supplies must be airlifted in. According to a *Time* report, under the circumstances, only about four thousand troops can be brought in per month. The Afghanistan surge is intended to stabilize population centers.

I understand the enormous pressure that President Obama is under to regain control of Afghanistan. Allowing the country to disintegrate is not an option—especially in light of the geography, which places it alongside Pakistan and Iran. The border with Pakistan, where al-Qaeda is hunkered down, stretches more than sixteen hundred miles across inhospitable, mountainous terrain. As a matter of perspective, we have been unable to secure a two-thousand-mile border with Mexico.

The importance of Pakistan in the fight against al-Qaeda cannot be understated. If Pakistan is committed to rooting out al-Qaeda, we should not be shy about financing that effort and also supplying them with the military hardware necessary without upsetting the balance of power in the region between Pakistan and India.

Newsweek reported, "During a long Sunday meeting with President Obama and top national-security advisers on Sept. 13, 2009, the VP [Joe Biden] interjected, 'Can I just clarify a factual point? How much will we spend this year on Afghanistan?' Someone provided the figure: $65 billion. 'And how much will we spend on Pakistan?' Another figure was supplied: $2.25 billion. 'Well, by my calculations that's a 30-to-1 ratio in favor of Afghanistan. So I have a question. Al-Qaeda is almost all in Pakistan, and Pakistan has nuclear weapons. And yet for every dollar we're spending in Pakistan, we're spending $30 in Afghanistan. Does that make strategic sense?' The White House Situation Room fell silent. But the questions had their desired effect: those gathered began putting more thought into Pakistan as the key theater in the region."

While some past Pakistani efforts to root out al-Qaeda have appeared halfhearted because of support for al-Qaeda in the ranks, more recently the Pakistan Army has been much more aggressive. Tragically, in response, in December 2009, al-Qaeda bombed a mosque where soldiers worshiped, killing thirty-six soldiers and family members.

I believe President Obama is absolutely committed to hunting down al-Qaeda, and if the Pakistan Army does not go after them in Pakistan, we will. This is tricky political terrain. . . . While the use of unmanned drones to target al-Qaeda along the border is already very unpopular, a full-fledged military operation by the U.S. Army would be even more controversial.

According to a December 21, 2009, *Guardian* report, "American special forces have conducted multiple clandestine raids into Pakistan's tribal areas as part of a secret war in the border region. . . . A former NATO officer said the incursions, only one of which has been previously reported, occurred between 2003 and 2008, involved helicopter-borne elite soldiers stealing across the border at night, and were never declared to the Pakistani government."

This much is certain. Before we can give serious thought to getting out of Afghanistan, al-Qaeda must be so badly beaten it is no longer a threat to Afghanistan or Pakistan. Clearly, though, until that is accomplished, this administration's strategy will be one of relentless pursuit. "We know that Al-Qaeda and its extremist allies threaten us from different corners of the globe—from Pakistan but also from East Africa and Southeast Asia; from Europe and the Gulf," Obama said in 2009. "And that's why we're applying focused and relentless pressure on Al-Qaeda," he said. Tactics include improved intelligence-sharing, disruption of terrorism financing, and specific attacks on al-Qaeda's leaders.

Let there be no delusion: This mess won't be wrapped up neatly with pretty ribbons. Our involvement in Afghanistan, and hopefully that of the global community, may well be multigenerational. We need a long-term *global* commitment and strategy to help build, feed, and educate that country. And then we must be prepared to follow bin Laden and his supporters like the hounds of hell to every corner of this earth. Anyone considering an attack on America like the one we endured on 9/11 should understand from our example that their reward will be a miserable, sleepless life on the run, and ultimately death.

GETTING THE DRUG TRADE UNDER CONTROL

One of the major complications to stabilizing Afghanistan is finding a solution to the drug economy in that country. Again, *globally,* we and other nations have to arrive at a solution to the opium trade. If we don't address that problem, it will be difficult to make progress. The estimated $4 billion opium trade funds the Taliban and represents well over half of the country's gross domestic product.

Why not take a page out of the American agriculture playbook? Through the Conservation Reserve Program, we pay American farmers to take some marginal land out of production. It's good for wildlife, which flourishes; it stops erosion, keeps commodities markets from being saturated, and puts money in the pocket of the farmer. Why not simply pay the Afghan farmers more than they make growing opium?

We could very well diminish the strength of the Taliban and shut down a major heroin pipeline in the process.

UNFINISHED BUSINESS IN IRAQ

Now let's consider the unfinished business in Iraq, a preemptive war over fictional WMDs that has claimed the lives of more than four thousand American soldiers. That said, I hope for a successful outcome because I want what is best for my country. But no outcome should ever be used as justification for the deceit the Bush administration used to drum up support for an unnecessary war. I'm glad that Saddam Hussein is out of power—indeed, deceased. Now we have to do our best to see that he is not succeeded by someone worse.

President Obama's goal is for the U.S. combat mission to end in 2010, with a residual force of up to fifty thousand to remain through the following year. General David Petraeus, head of the U.S. Central Command, warned in 2009 that "the progress there is still fragile and reversible."

We should harbor no illusions that our soldiers will leave behind any kind of utopia. However, if we can achieve stability in Iraq, we should aggressively help to rebuild the infrastructure through humanitarian efforts. In fact, those efforts will help achieve stability. Again, just as in Afghanistan, I'm talking about a multigenerational effort to improve relations between America and the Iraqi people.

We need to transform the way we think about war. Seemingly, we budget for the destruction, but we fail to properly budget for the cleanup. Instead of just looking for ways to feed the military industrial complex and the military's insatiable need for weaponry, let's take a percentage or two from that budget and set it aside to clean up the messes we have made. If we shifted even 1 percent from our military budget to humanitarian causes, what a message that would send to the rest of the world. We need to balance might with what is right. (It sounds a little like something Jesse Jackson might say, doesn't it? But I believe it.) Not only does it make sense from a moral perspective, it makes military sense. All too often we look at the perceived cost of humanitarian aid, without considering the bargain it is when measured against the cost of conflict.

AN IRAN PLAN

Now let's take a look at some other global players with whom we have to reckon.

Iran continues to make headlines with its nuclear program. The good news is, Russia seemed to be as concerned as we are about a secret Iranian facility that was revealed in 2009. The amount of leverage that nuclear weapons give a nation is reason enough for existing nuclear powers to want to discourage proliferation. The more fingers on the button, the greater the risk. There is no doubt in my mind that Iran is using the threat that it may acquire nuclear weapons as negotiating leverage, just as North Korea has. Just having the potential for nuclear weapons gives a country a great deal of leverage.

Newsweek columnist Fareed Zakaria advises, "We should not fear to negotiate with these rulers. [But] the ultimate solution to the problem of Iran will lie in an Iranian regime that understands it has much to gain from embracing the modern world. That doesn't mean Iran would forswear its efforts to be a regional power . . . but it does mean that Iran would be more willing to be open and transparent, and to demonstrate its peaceful intentions. It would view trade and contact with the West as a virtue, not a threat. It would return Iran to its historic role as a crossroads of commerce and capitalism, as one of the most sophisticated trading states in history, and a place where cultures mingled to produce dazzling art, architecture, poetry, and prose. This Iran would have its issues with the West, but it would not be a rogue regime, funding terrorists and secretly breaking its international agreements."

Certainly the hard-line approach of turning the Israeli Air Force loose to bomb Iranian nuclear facilities is a temporary solution akin to knocking a hornet's nest down in your garage. You end up with a bunch of ticked-off hornets looking to sting in all directions.

It's important that this doesn't turn into a United States vs. Iran issue, but one that includes the voices of the international community. I don't think we should be too hasty with sanctions. More moderate leadership may well emerge in Iran in time. Severe sanctions would undermine support for the United States among the Iranian people.

Azadeh Moaveni, a *Time* reporter, wrote in the *Washington Post* in June 2008, "Although their leaders still call America the Great Satan . . . [it] might startle some Americans to realize that Iran has one of the most pro-American populations in the Middle East. Iranians have adored America for nearly three decades, a sentiment rooted in nostalgia for Iran's golden days, before the worst of the shah's repression and the 1979 Islamic revolution." Still, Moaveni says, "President Bush's post-9/11 wars of liberation on both of Iran's borders—in Iraq to the west and Afghanistan to the east—rattled ordinary Iranians, and Washington's opposition to Iran's nuclear program—a major source of national pride—added to their resentment."

Of course, another underlying issue and leading cause of anti-American sentiment and suspicion in the Middle East is the Israeli-Palestinian issue, specifically our support for Israel, which is viewed as our proxy in the Middle East.

In the long run, can Obama do what every other president has failed to do—succeed in brokering peace and a Palestinian homeland in the Middle East? If so, a new era of relative global peace might be ushered in. However, this is something no American president alone can deliver. The Palestinians and the Israelis must both want peace badly enough. What Obama can do is help improve our image in the Middle East, which is no easy task, especially considering the potential for boots on the ground in Pakistani territory.

WHAT ABOUT RUSSIA?

And what about Russia? While politically the country has shown a willingness to be every bit as cantankerous as the old Soviet Union, internally
the standard of living has declined, despite the country's role as a global
energy superpower. We may not be able to comprehend it, but there is
still yearning among some Russians for the "old days" under a more stable communist system. As a newcomer to capitalism, the country is grappling with a disparity in wealth, and with crime and corruption.

Janusz Bugajski, director of the New European Democracies program at the Center for Strategic and International Studies, wrote in an
opinion in the *Washington Times:* "Russia remains a serious threat to its
weaker neighbors, irrespective of its structural and fiscal weaknesses and
overdependence on hydrocarbon revenues. Moscow continues to engage
in a policy of subversion and destabilization across the former Soviet
empire, especially through its control of vital energy resources."

It will be a test for the Obama administration to try to relax tensions
between the United States and our old adversary. Certainly, dismantling
the missile shield sent a positive signal. If Russia joins the United States
and other countries in negotiating an agreement with Iran on the nuclear
issue, it could go a long way toward elevating Russia's stature and improving its relations with the West. Also, when it comes to Afghanistan, Russia
should be encouraged to take a role in stabilizing the country—after
all, they spent twenty years destroying it.

While these issues cannot be solved in the course of one administration, I believe that President Obama's overall direction is correct. That's
why it will be crucial that America continues to elect like-minded individuals in the future. In my perfect world, Barack Obama serves two
successful terms and then makes way for another Democratic administration.

While George W. Bush may have broken more in eight years than
can be fixed in that same time frame, many of the underlying issues have

been brewing for decades—centuries, even. Those plotting the course today will not live long enough to see the eventual destination, but it doesn't make the cause any less urgent or noble.

Plans and intentions all look good on paper. The reality most administrations discover is that *events* dictate the direction of presidencies more often than presidencies dictate events. It's like being the bartender on a Saturday night—the chances of an uneventful evening are slim.

CHAPTER EIGHT

BAD TRADE

Selling Out the American Worker

THE FIRST SHOT IN DEFENSE OF THE AMERICAN WORKER WAS FIRED by Barack Obama in September 2009 when he put a tariff on Chinese tires. Some 46 million tires in 2008 alone not only put Chinese rubber on the roads, they put American workers on the streets, as the Chinese share of the U.S. tire market grew from 4.7 percent in 2004 to 16.7 percent by 2008, from 14.6 million to 46 million tires.

As reported in the *Wall Street Journal,* four U.S. tire plants closed in 2006 and 2007 and more than 5,100 workers lost their jobs. Three more plants were in the process of shutting down, which would put another 3,000 workers out of a job.

This "dumping" was yet another in a line of trade violations perpetrated on the United States, but for the first time in a long time, an American president stood up for American workers.

Leo Gerard, president of USW (United Steel Workers), which brought the suit against the Chinese, wrote on the *Huffington Post* in mid-September 2009, "Don't kid yourself. This is a battle. . . . The U.S. economy is under attack by countries engaging in unfair trade. In the past decade, we've lost 40,000 manufacturing facilities. . . . Since the Great

Recession began, more than 2 million manufacturing workers have lost their jobs, making their unemployment rate 11.8 percent."

While all eyes were on Wall Street and the investment bank shenanigans that triggered an economic heart attack in the economy, most people didn't realize that there was an underlying cancer eating away at America, which had weakened us and made us more vulnerable to an economic crisis.

THE RIDICULOUS REWARDS WE GIVE OUTSOURCERS

North Dakota senator Byron Dorgan, a Democrat, detailed the insidious way bad trade deals and bad policy are rewarding the turncoat companies that ship jobs overseas in his book *Take This Job and Ship It:* "When a U.S. company closes down a U.S. manufacturing plant, fires its American workers and moves those good-paying jobs to China or other locations abroad . . . the tax code allows these firms to defer paying any U.S. income taxes on the earnings from those new foreign-manufactured products until those profits are returned, if ever, to this country." Contrarily, a domestic manufacturer "is required to pay immediate U.S. taxes on the profits it earns here." Dorgan proposed legislation to close the tax loophole, which would not only save jobs but save taxpayers $15 billion over ten years. Sadly, the American worker will lose Dorgan's voice in Congress. He has announced that he will not run for reelection in 2010.

When it comes to bad policy, the North American Free Trade Agreement was a whopper. NAFTA alone increased the trade deficit with Mexico and Canada from $9.1 billion to $138.5 billion between 1994 and 2007, according to the Center for International Policy. The net loss in jobs attributed to NAFTA was almost a million.

Bad trade agreements are at the core of the problem, and when countries like China violate trade agreements, it begins to erode the economy even faster. Part of the problem with these bad trade deals is the indifference and ignorance of the American consumer and international businesses like Walmart, whose drive to squeeze every last penny of profit from each transaction has been pursued at the expense of the American worker.

No, this won't be another long-winded harangue about the evils of Walmart. I documented that in my last book, and Senator Dorgan and a host of others have dissected the issue even more thoroughly in theirs. But when the world's largest retailer exploits the global job market to buy goods as cheaply as possible, and American consumers go along with it, it truly becomes, as I've mentioned before, a race to the bottom line. American manufacturing jobs go to China.

"The simple reality is that what these trade policies are about—and [they] have been forced upon us by large multinational corporations—they are asking American workers to compete against desperate people in the developing world, who in some cases make pennies an hour," said Senator Bernie Sanders (I-VT) in a statement in 2007, which can still be found on his website. "And if you are a large corporate leader, it doesn't take a Ph.D. in economics to understand that, yes, you will throw American workers out on the street, who make $20 an hour, have health care, and where you have to obey environmental regulations. And yes, you'll run to China, pay people 30 cents an hour. If they stand up for a union, they go to jail. If they stand up for environmental regulations, they go to jail. Why wouldn't you go to China? And of course, that's exactly what many, many American corporations are doing."

The Department of Labor reports that the U.S. manufacturing sector lost 791,000 people in 2008 and 4 million manufacturing jobs since 2000. Unemployment rises. With a glut of workers available, it becomes an employer's market. Employers can keep wages down. Wages stagnate. From 2000 to 2007, according the U.S. Commerce Department, the median income actually fell by $324. Thanks, Dubya. But I guess those tax cuts for the richest of the rich worked out OK for them, didn't they? Hey, will someone please remind them to trickle down?

With so many American factories shuttered and so many jobs lost to the Great Recession, what happens? The unemployed and underemployed start to put more pressure on social programs. They stress the health care system. They get food stamps. Fuel assistance. Your taxes rise. Why? Because you are subsidizing underpaid Walmart employees and the people in international corporations that profited by putting Americans out of work. What drives me crazy is that Republicans, who spent the last decade cheerleading outsourcing, now complain about the added pressures the unemployed are putting on social programs. I don't think it is simple hypocrisy—most of them just don't get it! The rest don't care.

Here's an example of how the deck is stacked against American manufacturers. In 2006, according to the *New York Times,* only 5,000 American cars were sold in South Korea, because of trade barriers. Meanwhile, 800,000 South Korean cars were sold in America. Even more ominously, the U.S. auto industry is bracing for Chinese cars, which will be test marketed in other countries before hitting the U.S. market within five years. GS Motors, a Mexican company, imports the cars from China's First Auto Works—4,000 in 2008—but expects the cars to be built in Mexico by 2010. The cars sell for $5,500. Is Detroit in any condition to withstand any meaningful pressure from Chinese/Mexican automakers? I don't know the answer, but I do know that if the cars are allowed to flood the market, Detroit may be sunk.

Among the industries in America that are virtually extinct is the garment industry, once the largest employer in America. Today, according to the HBO documentary *Schmatta: Rags to Riches to Rags,* 95 percent of all garments sold in the U.S. are made mostly in sweatshops in China, Vietnam, and Bangladesh.

When Levi Strauss, which had employed 37,000 American workers, moved its operations to China in 2003, Clara Flores, an employee of the company for twenty-four years and president of the plant's union, told the *New York Times* that the $18-an-hour job and benefits would be hard to replace. Marivel Gutierez, another twenty-four-year employee, told the *Times*, "There still probably is an American dream. But what about us? What happens to our American dream?"

It's obvious that when trade policy is constructed in America, the focus is on what's good for international corporations and not the American worker. The American worker is not regarded as a flesh-and-blood human being, a mother, a father, a son, or daughter. No! You are an expense, an impediment to profit.

WE DESERVE SOME OF THE BLAME

As American consumers, we have encouraged this behavior because we're like shoppers at a shady pawnshop. We don't want to know the story behind the goods; we just want them cheap. It's cool until you get your pink slip. It doesn't matter *until it matters*. You have to ask yourself, How much am I really saving when I don't buy American?

For eight years we heard the mantra "Support the troops," despite Republican efforts to cut troop pay, their votes against funding the VA, and stop-loss programs. Damn right we should support the troops, but while we're at it, let's start putting up ribbons for the American Worker, too. We ought to tie a blood-red ribbon on every tree and light pole in America to signify the jobs shipped overseas. I'm serious. It'll be good for the ribbon business. I hear they're on sale at Walmart.

The trade deficit in 2008 was $677 billion, which, due to a floundering economy in the second half of the year, was actually down from $700 billion in 2007. One word you will hear from economists about the deficit is that it is "unsustainable." Peter Morici, a former director of economics at the U.S. International Trade Commission, said in February 2009, "To finance the deficit of recent years, Americans have borrowed more than $6.5 trillion from foreign sources, including foreign governments, and the debt service comes to more than $1,500 for each working American."

This transfer of wealth from America to the Chinese and the Middle East (oil accounts for $450 billion of the trade deficit) gives these countries the ability to buy up America piece by piece—real estate, stocks, bonds, and businesses. *Translation:* If we don't buy Ameri*can,* they buy Ameri*ca.*

The Bureau of Economic Analysis reports that foreign investors own more of America than American investors own of the rest of the world. *Fortune* magazine's Geoff Colvin wrote in 2008 that as foreign ownership grows, "we must send more dividends and interest to foreign owners, giving them more money with which to buy more U.S. assets, earning more dividends, and so on." I don't want to sound like Lou Dobbs with hemorrhoids, but we need to be talking about this issue now. At what point do we draw the line?

It is just one of many reasons for making the trade deficit more manageable, but the key to our economic resurgence is the awesome power the engine of job growth can provide. After World War II, with favorable economic conditions, the middle class grew and thrived, becoming the backbone of an economic juggernaut.

So even though the stimulus package has boosted the U.S. economy and job retention and growth, one of the main drags on the economy— the trade deficit—will have to be addressed in order for the U.S. economy to recover in the long term. Otherwise, Morici warns, "a pattern of false recoveries, much as occurred during the Great Depression, will likely emerge. Conditions will not be as bad, and unemployment will stay at unacceptable levels."

When it comes to trade, the Chinese do not play Ping-Pong. They play hardball. According to Senator Dorgan, China has pressured Boeing, saying that if they want to sell planes to China they must open a factory there. It sounds like something you'd hear from the Mob.

I wrote earlier in this book that America never seems to muster the will to react until it perceives a crisis. The trade deficit is a crisis, but it is subversively quiet—it's like slowly bleeding to death. It hurts a little at first, then you get sleepy . . . and then you wake up dead. I believe the Obama administration understands how important this issue is to America's future. However, there are many supporters of free trade who are seemingly oblivious to the harm the agreements have done to American workers. There will be millions and billions of corporate lobbying dollars spent to fight what they will brand protectionism and I will call survival.

SETTING GOALS

Our goal should be to cut the trade deficit by half in the next decade—and that may be too modest a proposal. Meeting such a goal will require a national focus on energy independence, since that is a huge part of the problem. When it comes to other imports, we will need to exhibit the same kind of toughness Obama showed on the tire issue. By all means, let us encourage trade, but we no longer need to treat all of our partners like ninety-eight-pound weaklings. Those with mature, robust economies cannot be allowed entry into our market without extending the same invitation to U.S. exporters.

I recognize that trade is necessary. I also recognize that unless we renegotiate bad treaties and enforce the laws of existing ones, we cannot hope to have a stable economy. Trade wars serve no purpose, but we have to stick up for the American worker and give the American manufacturer an even playing field. Obama has already taken the first step, which is to *enforce* trade agreements. Second, we must renegotiate NAFTA and other suspect agreements. Third, we have to amend U.S. tax laws so that we stop rewarding companies who outsource and start punishing those who do.

Finally, we have to address the issue of international currency "fixing." As discussed in the chapter on China, by keeping its yuan pegged artificially low to the dollar, China's goods remain attractively priced in the U.S. market and American products are at a price disadvantage. Specifically, the Obama administration has to follow through on its challenge to China over currency manipulation.

This is all eminently doable, but it will not come without fits and starts and bumps in the road as each trading partner negotiates for the best possible advantage. I'm not sure who has negotiated some of these past treaties, but if his name was Curly, Larry, or Moe, I wouldn't be shocked.

IT'S ABOUT BASIC HUMAN RIGHTS

At its core, the whole issue of outsourcing is really a reflection of the value we put on human dignity and human rights. Ultimately, if we are to stop this devastating race to the bottom, we have to include in these agreements workplace protection and economic standards for workers in emerging economies, just as unions did in America.

Rather than forcing American workers to compete in the gutter, this serves the purpose of elevating abused workers, including child laborers, in other countries. Under no circumstances should we be encouraging and enabling workplace abuses in other countries by allowing the import of goods produced in that manner.

According to the International Labor Organization, there are an estimated 250 million children, ages five to fourteen, working in hazardous conditions. Senator Bernie Sanders said, "Most of us would be horrified to support a business that exploits children. But chances are you may have done just that on your last shopping trip. Perhaps you splurged on a handcrafted carpet, without knowing it was made by a seven-year-old from India, where children are chained to looms for 12 hours a day. Maybe you just bought a soccer ball for your son or daughter, without realizing five-year-old hands inside a dark and silent factory in Pakistan produced your gift. . . . Children's rights groups estimate that the U.S. imports more than $100 million in goods each year which are produced by bonded and indentured children."

When we, as a country, import products produced by child labor, it says as much about our moral standards as it does about those who enslave children.

According to Reuters, "the annual cotton harvest in Uzbekistan depends on the forced labor of some 2.7 million children, who are all removed from school for six to eight weeks to work in the fields and enrich the elites of the country's authoritarian regime." The story quotes a new study, *Invisible to the World: The Dynamics of Forced Child Labour in the Cotton Sector of Uzbekistan:* "Uzbekistan represents a rare instance of state-sanctioned mass mobilization of children's labour. The principal beneficiaries are not households or primary producers, but state-controlled trading companies."

As a response to child labor abuses, the U.S. Labor Department, with $92 million allocated in 2010, funds 220 projects in 82 countries to address the issue. Compare that to the Bush administration, which proposed a $66 million *cut,* to $15 million, in 2008. Congress, instead, allocated $91 million.

It's important that our trade agreements reflect similar environmental standards, too. No more allowing into our playpens the flood of Chinese toys with lead paint. Nor can we allow crops treated with chemicals banned in the United States to appear on our shelves from other countries. What message do we send and what is the cost to American manufacturers when we import Chinese goods made in plants that do not have to adhere to the same pollution standards we have in America? In the end, the pollution from the very same Chinese manufacturing plants that put Americans out of work floats over American cities.

Trade can be a powerful tool for improving lives in America and abroad, but the benefits have to be balanced among the businesses that should make a profit, the employees, and the overall health of the economies of all countries involved.

All negotiators ought to know when they sit down that their goal is to benefit America as a whole, not just one sector at the expense of another. Trade agreements influenced by the corporate traders themselves, as has been the case, have led us down the wrong path, to shuttered factories, unemployment, and stagnant wages in America.

CHAPTER NINE

ECONOMIC SLAVERY

How Debt Reductions and Unions
Can Help Set You Free

I WANT TO TALK ABOUT FREEDOM FOR A MOMENT. NOT THE DRA-matic "let my people go" freedom but rather the personal freedom that comes with making smart personal decisions. You live in the land of the free, but are you really free? If you are underwater on your mortgage and facing $1,200 health insurance premiums, payments on that Hummer you just had to have, credit cards maxed out, and a 401(k) that's going south in a hurry, well then, freedom isn't all its cracked up to be, is it?

I remember when I was growing up the television commercials warning about shady drug dealers and how they would get you hooked in a heartbeat. But no one ever warned us about the guys in the suits offering instant gratification. Buy now, pay later! Easy credit!

Don't get me wrong. Credit can be a wonderful tool for improving your quality of life. But too much debt limits your choices in life. As Ralph Waldo Emerson said, "A man in debt is so far a slave."

The way I see it, being debt-free and having something socked away for a rainy day offers peace of mind—and peace of mind is invaluable. Isn't peace of mind the point of it all? Unfortunately, this materialistic generation has been slow to learn. We really are the Greediest Generation. We're working so hard to weed the roses that we no longer stop to smell them.

In the rush to own flat-panel big-screen TVs and BMWs, people soon discover that those things start owning *them*. The monthly payments demand you get up each day to pay for it all—sometimes at a job you don't like. I believe you have to love what you do to be successful at it. I also believe there ought to be some joy in our lives. It's just hard to get there if you've created your own economic prison and a cycle of living from paycheck to paycheck.

It's easy to point fingers and complain about the inequities in the system, but ultimately, you have to take responsibility for your actions. I'm an old-school, pull-yourself-up-by-your-bootstraps kind of guy. I admire a good work ethic, and I believe in working hard to achieve what I want to achieve. That's what America is all about.

I have spent a good deal of time taking the system to task because a combination of deregulation and corruption has put too much power in too few hands. Capitalism often operates without regard to human rights and justice, and I think the system needs to better address those issues. Despite that, I embrace the risk/reward concept of capitalism.

I believe in paying my way, and I respect those who own up to bad decisions and pay their debts instead of taking the easy way out and declaring bankruptcy. But it seems to me that this generation has gotten fiscally sloppy—personally and as a nation. We have been so busy hedonistically living for today, we have not thought much about the future.

I remember even as child looking around and recognizing that some of the adults in my world were working at jobs they detested. Others found fulfillment in theirs. I resolved then to find an occupation that would make me happy and would make me feel at the end of the day that I had made a difference. I have been blessed to have that, but along with the blessings came an awful lot of work.

This is what I tell my children: Manage your debt. Love what you do. Work for yourself if you can. Stick up for yourself by joining a union if you want to work for someone else. And through it all, leave the world a better place.

DON'T DIG A HOLE DEEPER THAN
YOU CAN CRAWL OUT OF

The first advice I would give to any young person starting out is to be wary of debt. You are entering the job market at a most inhospitable time, so try not to exacerbate the situation by taking on too much *unnecessary debt*. There are two kinds of debt—necessary and unnecessary—but only you can define what is necessary for you and your circumstance.

No one really knows if the American economy will continue to churn out jobs at the rate it has historically. I'm optimistic, but economists are all over the map because with outsourcing and the vagaries of trade policy and global economics, we are in uncharted territory. After the first George Bush recession, the jobs lagged far behind, and that is what many predict will happen this time. Hope for the best but prepare for the worst.

The New Normal may well include higher unemployment. Rutgers economists Joseph Seneca and James Hughes say even Clintonesque job growth at 2.4 million a year would still mean unemployment numbers wouldn't fall to 5 percent until 2017. That's partly because, as the population grows, the labor force expands by a million annually. The job market may be further squeezed if those near retirement age, whose 401(k)s have evaporated, decide they have to keep working a few more years. It's not an easy time to be joining the workforce.

Well, when the going gets tough, the tough get going.

As ruthless as it may sound, during a recession blood flows in the streets, and that's when the sharks make money. It's better to be the shark instead of the meal. There are opportunities in every economy, and it's the action of the risk taker that sparks economic revival. If you see an opportunity to start your own business, do your homework, and then go for it.

Here's where *necessary* debt comes in. If you have completed a business plan, imagined every worst-case scenario, and it still pencils out, then that's the time to start talking to a lender—maybe even investors. Whatever you do, don't take a step until you know which direction you are going. A well-thought-out business plan is the key.

I have been pushing hard for the president and Congress to make available low-interest loans with favorable terms to small businesses—that is where the long-term stability of the economy will come from. It is about diversity. It's a way of hedging our bets. Why plow billions into Wall Street and ignore Main Street? Think about it. We're investing in the American economy. Let's use a time-tested economic investment strategy and diversify!

Did you know that slightly more than half of the jobs in this country are provided by small businesses? According to the Small Business Administration, that's about 30 million jobs. I've called for a small business czar to put the focus on job creation through small business expansion, so I was pleased when President Obama announced the formation of the Task Force on Middle Class Working Families, led by Vice President Joe Biden, to find the best ways to create jobs, improve workplace safety, and pursue other policies that benefit the middle class. I would add to the agenda finding a way to cut through all the SBA red tape and put loans to small businesses on a fast track. Small business owners who have tried to work with the Small Business Administration know how slow and unwieldy the process is.

And how about a stimulus package for the people on the ground floor of growing this economy? Give them incentives! Cheap loans with favorable terms! Zero interest for five years! That's how we can put Americans back to work again.

It's too early to know how much impact Joe Biden's task force will have, but he's a good man with blue-collar roots, and I think the president needs more of that blue-collar background in the White House. In Washington, when billion-dollar industries start to collapse, it gets everyone's attention. So the president has wisely put big business experts like Treasury Secretary Tim Geithner and economic advisor Larry Summers around him to help steady the economy.

But where is the guy in the administration who has sat up in bed at 3 A.M. in a cold sweat wondering if he can meet payroll, wondering if he is going to have to lay off workers? The president needs someone who has been in those trenches to advise him.

I'm serious as a heart attack about this. Washington sees the big picture, but unless you have been in the trenches on Main Street—where the most potential for job growth is—you cannot possibly know how to jump-start small business growth. I am sometimes dismayed when I talk to senators, congresspeople, and other Washington officials because they often don't have a clue about the obstacles small business owners face. That's because we have morphed from what was supposed to be a citizen government into one that is comprised of professional politicians who, as well meaning as they may be, are out of touch. Sure, get me Larry Summers, but get me Larry the Cable Guy, too.

That ought to make for an interesting conversation.

RETHINKING CAREER PATHS

Some jobs cannot be outsourced. Plumbers, electricians, mechanics, and carpenters are in demand and well paid. You want to make a good living and enjoy some job security? Consider the trades. The schools are often cheaper, and there is an opportunity to work for yourself, which I highly recommend. I think we are dug into a mind-set that the only real success in this world comes through wearing a suit and a tie. That couldn't be farther than the truth.

I speak from experience. My sons operate E. A. Schultz Construction—our small company that pours concrete and can build pretty much anything you need built. Joe and Christian work hard on the job sites—it's backbreaking, physical labor, but if they choose to, someday they can take what they have learned in the trenches and apply that to management or even ownership. The best managers and owners in the world are the ones who have done every tough, dirty job in the business. If you've walked the walk, you can damn sure talk the talk.

I have worked for some of the biggest media groups in the country, and I always worked hard because I took pride in being the best employee in the building—and when I created my own businesses, I worked even harder. My work ethic will never be the reason I fail. I may make mistakes, I may get a bad break, but I won't ever fail because I didn't try hard enough. In fact, the way I see it, as long as I keep trying, I will eventually succeed. It's about seeking excellence. You can't half-ass it in this life.

I talk about an economic "New Normal" in this book—a world of suppressed wages, of peons and kings, and when you look at the imbalance of wealth in the nation and in the world, the evidence is there that this is what has happened, but that doesn't mean we should stop trying. It means we have to try harder. Forget about the odds and the statistics. One bright mind and a strong work ethic can rise above all that. We have got to become as tough as the times in which we live. The key to survival is excellence. That, and voting in your own self-interest.

WHY WE NEED UNIONS

Not everyone is cut out to operate his or her own business, but working for someone else leaves workers vulnerable. That's where unions come in. Without unions, the working conditions in America would be as bad as they are today in emerging economies around the world.

The working conditions in Chinese factories remain abysmal—in some cases, a death sentence. Reporter Loretta Tofani, who spent fourteen months in China researching workplace conditions, returned with a report to *PBS NewsHour* in 2007 that featured photographs of workers in oxygen tents dying from inhaling metal particles, pictures of workers spraying lead paint with no masks on, and others with missing fingers.

There is a cancer epidemic in the making in China. Tofani said, "I found that there were carcinogens being used by people, by the workers, in a really extravagant manner. People were spraying benzenes. There were people who had silicosis from making our metal goods. And it would seem like it was in every industry. It was furniture. It was shoes, clothes, marble tiles, granite countertops. Virtually every industry went through this system, where workers were living and breathing in carcinogens or using machines that were unguarded and resulted in amputations."

Why is this allowed to continue? In China, unions are forbidden.

Unions were instrumental in building the American middle class—an economic machine the likes of which the world had never before seen. There is no doubt in my mind that without unions, this would be a much different country. In this book I have mentioned countries with no labor standards where children as young as five are put to work. If you go back in American history, you'll discover child labor was once common here, too.

But late in the nineteenth century, unions appeared to defend the American worker. The most famous of them was the American Federation of Labor, founded by Samuel Gompers. At its peak, the AFL had 1.4 million members who sought child labor laws, workplace safety, a shorter workday, and fair wages. In short, what they sought, Gompers said, was "more school houses and less jails. More books and less guns. More learning and less vice. More leisure and less greed. More justice and less revenge. We want more . . . opportunities to cultivate our better natures."

I remember reading about Samuel Gompers in school without ever grasping what a transformational figure he was. When he died in 1924, the world he left behind was on its way to becoming a much better place. What Gompers and other labor organizers did was to literally emancipate the American worker. Furthermore, I believe that the revolution in the workplace set the stage for women's rights and civil rights, too. They are all human rights issues. When it comes to human rights, if we are not advancing, we are backsliding.

For decades, because of the power of the unions, the middle class in America prospered, but that all began to change with globalization. The country adopted trade agreements that rewarded outsourcing and embraced a policy of indifference toward illegal immigration. Corporations brazenly turned the clock back on all the hard-fought gains unions had won over the years by moving factories overseas where unions were illegal and labor standards virtually nonexistent. Cheap labor flooded in from Mexico, and suddenly the incomes of middle-class Americans stagnated . . . stopped dead in their tracks. That's where we are today.

The crazy thing is that this new generation of CEOs doesn't get how important—how crucial—the middle class is. They seem to think they can continue to ship American jobs overseas with no consequences. They forget that the workforce is comprised of the very same people who make up the marketplace. It's an insane economic model that works only for a small, greedy few for a short while and is destined to wreak havoc on society as a whole. They just don't get that what's good for the middle class is good for the country.

The good news is that labor now has a friend in the White House.

"The strength of our economy can be measured directly by the strength of the middle class," Obama said when he announced the aforementioned Middle Class Task Force. "I do not view the Labor Movement as part of the problem. To me, it is part of the solution. . . . We need to level the playing field for workers and the unions that represent their interest. . . . When workers are prospering, they buy products that make businesses prosper."

The American form of government is predicated on checks and balances. That's what unions are—a check to the power of corporations. That's why a resurgence of the labor movement at this moment in history

is critical. While tax loopholes that reward outsourcing are closed and illegal labor restricted, it is equally important that a worker's right to join a
union be free of intimidation by ownership.

I support the Employee Free Choice Act, a bill that would do just
that.

Under the current system, corporations have learned to stall and intimidate those who would start a union. The Employee Free Choice Act
moves the process along more quickly and fairly. If the process stalls,
arbitrators are called in. Those on the wrong side of the issue have created a hullabaloo because the act shifts some leverage from ownership to
the worker.

Corporate opposition to this has been strong, and why wouldn't it
be? Even as productivity has risen, corporations have managed to sup-
press wages. Lower overhead means higher profits and a windfall for
owners and stockholders—what's not to love if you're at the top of the
food chain? According to economist Jagdish Bhagwati, from 2000 to
2007, "virtually *all* of the nation's economic growth went to a small number of wealthy Americans." The problem? "The erosion of workers'
ability to form unions and bargain collectively."

According to the AFL-CIO, "Union members are 52 percent more
likely to have job-provided health care, nearly three times more likely to
have guaranteed pensions and earn 28 percent more than nonunion
workers."

The Employee Free Choice Act *does* play hardball. But you know
what? These are hard times. Don't weep for Big Business. Ownership
will always have the advantage. *Always.* If workers cannot organize freely,
they don't stand a chance. Freedom . . . Fairness . . . That's what this is
all about. We want a little more of the profit to go from the CEOs to the
guys busting their asses on the factory floor. These folks aren't asking for
anything more than a fair shake.

According to the Institute for Policy Studies and United for a Fair
Economy, the ratio of compensation between CEOs and workers in

2005 was to be 411 to 1. This is the direct result of the Republican trickle-down mind-set ushered in by Ronald Reagan in 1980. Back then, according to the *Economist,* the CEO-worker ratio was only 40 to 1. If you're a workingman or workingwoman who votes Republican, don't you have to look at a statistic like that and wonder why you are voting against your best interests?

STOCK MARKET PERVERSIONS PUT AMERICAN WORKERS ON THE STREET

Let's talk for a moment about stockholder expectations and publicly traded corporations. In the last thirty years it seems to me we have been accelerating toward greed and away from economic fundamentals, and it is another nail in the coffin of the middle-class worker.

The system used to make sense. A company sold stock to raise capital for expansion and innovation. The money funded research and new products, which in turn legitimately increased the value of the stock. Ideally, the company expanded and more workers were added to the payroll. That's the way it's *supposed* to work. And there was a time in the not so distant past when a veteran of the stock market could advise you to simply buy good stock and hold it. But that just doesn't seem to be true anymore.

Stock prices are hard to predict, it seems to me, because we have veered so far away from the basics. You could probably do just as well by going to the track and betting on the prettiest pony.

Before technology stocks tanked in 2000, investors were like the Dutch speculating on tulip bulbs—with no rhyme or reason. In 1637, tulip contracts sold for ten times as much as the wage of the average craftsman. In 1998, we were happily investing in companies that were hemorrhaging money. Many people holding tech stocks in the 1990s became wealthy on paper, but ended up bloodied. Just before the crash someone asked Warren Buffett if he should sell a stock that had shot up in value, or if he should hold out for even higher gains. Buffett replied, "No one ever lost money by taking a profit."

If you invest in the market, remember that advice.

The goal has become to increase the value of the stock price, but as often as not, that effort has little relation to the productivity or direction of the company. Sure, there is a time and a place to bet on a new, innovative player, but most stocks are not worth what they are selling for. If you actually looked at the profit and earnings of each company, the real value of the stock market would be shrunken considerably—probably to about half of what it is today.

I know it is almost un-American to ask this question, but I will: *How much profit is enough?* Unreasonable stockholder expectations and corporate greed have combined to pervert entire industries. Even *very profitable* businesses have chosen to take advantage of cheap labor in China and India so they can make *even more* profit. The stockholder loves it, and the CEO gets giant bonuses, but what about the American worker? He or she is on the street.

If this isn't selling your soul, I don't know what is.

Remember, all profit comes at a price.

The sad fact is that there are lines of greedy people willing to sell out their fellow Americans for a few dollars more. If there is such a thing as economic treason, this is it.

In the push to inflate stock prices, workers become little more than part of an equation—being hired or fired to make the books look good in the short term, without any regard to the reality that these are human beings with families to raise and mortgages to pay. Ironically, with the advent of the 401(k), the workingman himself has become an investor, but paradoxically, what is good for him as an investor may not be good for him as a worker.

As investors, I think it's important that we become more accountable, too. There are moral decisions to be made. As investors, we can be part of the problem or part of the solution. If my 401(k) is holding

Halliburton stock, I don't want any part of it or any company that might put a dime in that son of a bitch Dick Cheney's pocket. I don't want to own any part of a company that uses child labor, and I damn sure don't want to invest a dime in any outsourcing bastards. I don't want to support bad corporate behavior, period!

There are millions of people who think like you and I do. There are "socially responsible" investment funds, some with very good track records. We know fair trade coffee sells when customers are given a choice. I know products made in the USA sell—even if they might cost a bit more. People will always support something they believe in. Surely, if enough people start investing only in companies they find ethical, it could begin to change the way other companies do business. Believe me, if there is more money in wearing a white hat instead of a black one, they'll do it.

CHAPTER TEN

THE TRUTH ABOUT TAXES

Time for Mandatory Trickling

IT'S TIME TO PAY THE PIPER, BUT THERE WILL NOT BE ANY DANCING to the music. As the federal debt creeps toward $12 trillion, with the 2009 deficit projected to be $1.75 trillion, with *one third* of our expenditures going to satisfy the *interest* on the debt, America is in danger of becoming a giant banana republic.

There seems to be this phenomenal case of amnesia sweeping the nation as to how we got here, and if you bring it up, well, they say you're just playing the blame game. But telling the truth isn't the same as placing blame.

It was a supposed tax-and-spend Democrat, Bill Clinton, who turned over the U.S. economy to George W. Bush with four consecutive budget surpluses that had the country on track to pay off the debt by now. Bush inherited a $5 trillion debt, but it was on the decline. However, with reckless spending that included the Medicare Drug Bill, a $1.2 trillion expense over a decade, according to the *Washington Post,* that Bush claimed would cost less than $400 billion, Bush ruined Clinton's good work. Talk about a royal scam! They knew the bill was a budget buster, but they wanted to secure the vote of the most consistent voters—

senior citizens. Then came two tax cuts for the richest Americans—$2.5 trillion from 2001 to 2010, according to Citizens for Tax Justice. Add to the mix the cost of the Iraq War, estimated to be as high as $3 trillion, according to economist James Stiglitz.

We had been moving forward.

Bush and his Republican enablers in Congress (a majority for six years) took us backward into financial disaster, spreading around another $700 billion to his Wall Street cronies on the way out.

Had Bush continued down Clinton's path, the debt would now be paid and the deficit eliminated. The last time that happened was in 1835 under Andrew Jackson.

So Barack Obama has been forced to do what most economists say has to be done—stimulate the economy when no one else is spending. That means even more debt.

Now that they don't have their hands on the checkbook, it is so disingenuous as to be laughable the way the Republicans have suddenly discovered fiscal responsibility. These born again Republicans have delayed the progress of government with procedural votes to slow key legislation, like extended unemployment benefits. In September 2009, what could have been passed in a day or two turned into an ordeal before the majority of Republicans voted for the unemployment extension—but only after receiving tax breaks for business in the package. While they stalled, 200,000 Americans that they had put out of work in the first place with their policies ran out of unemployment benefits. What is at stake? Power. By slowing the process, the Republicans want to claim, "See, we told you. Those guys can't get anything done!"

Apparently, you can't pass anything in Washington without giving Republican cronies a tax break. The formula is the same: Cut taxes. Well, I'm all for it. But let's cut taxes for the middle class. However, as Michael Moore pointed out in his movie *Capitalism: A Love Story,* since the top 1 percent owns 95 percent of the financial wealth (a figure confirmed by PolitiFact.org), they can afford to pay more. For the record, the top 1 percent pays about 40 percent of the federal taxes collected each year—but when you consider that they own 95 percent of the total wealth, that's hardly extreme.

We are in a system consisting of financial royalty and worker bees. There's a lot to be admired about worker bees, but who can truly say they are getting their fair share of the honey? Despite all the complaints from the American oligarchy about the transfer of wealth, the wealth has gone their way!

One way to keep government programs from growing is to blow up the national debt. Mission accomplished. The Republicans did just that and, in the process, stole the birthright of health care and education from the American people. They piled so much debt on the heads of our children that, for the first time ever, a generation of Americans will probably have a lower standard of living than the generation that preceded them. Every man, woman, and child's share of the national debt is in the neighborhood of $40,000.

It's a crime.

From the end of World War II until we hit the Reagan years, middle-class growth had exceeded that of every class. But by dismantling the rules that had protected the middle class, capitalism became legalized robbery. Credit card rates spiked; 401(k)s plunged. This oligarchy sucked money out of the system like vacuum cleaners. They got into every corner that was unregulated and got every dime they could.

Here's the thing most people miss. Specifically, I mean this is the thing *Republican voters* miss. They get distracted talking about taxes, without ever stopping to think about all the other ways that dollars are being drained from them. Oil companies get you at the pump. Ken Lay jacks up your utility bill. Insurance companies ratchet up the premiums and deny the coverage. Your investments founder on Wall Street. Credit card companies change the rules in midstream. This behavior is enabled by politicians who are bought off by these very same corporations.

When 1 percent enjoys 95 percent of the financial wealth, you don't have to worry about getting screwed by the taxman on April 15. You've been getting screwed all year long. Tell me, in what reasonable system does so much go to so few?

There are a couple of ways to get it back. Reinstate regulations and a level playing field to make capitalism competitive, or tax those greedy fat bastards back into the Stone Age! (Excuse me while I channel Curtis LeMay.) Actually, we need to do both—increase taxes on the wealthy, as well as regulate and break up monopolies.

Why not go to the heart of the problem? Congressman Peter Defazio has an idea I can get behind, and that is to tax stock market trades .25 percent. That would raise $150 billion for a Job Creation Reserve. Naturally, they screamed about this idea on Wall Street like stuck pigs. Billionaire Mark Cuban suggested on his blog in 2008: "Tax every single share of stock that is bought and sold 10 cents per transaction. One dime. If you buy a share of stock, your brokerage pays a 10 cent tax. If you sell a share, your brokerage pays a 10 cent tax. 1 share, 100 million shares. It's 10 cents per share. Of course, the tax will be paid for by those of us who are buying and selling stocks. So what. Here is the reality. If you are a true investor. Someone who wants to own a share of stock in a company you believe in, then it's an amount that is not going to impact your investment decision making process."

THE TAX CUT SHELL GAME

People also get distracted by federal income tax, never stopping to realize that when the feds cut taxes, the burden gets passed on to the state and school district. Property tax and local sales tax go up, and you pay anyway.

Paul Krugman, the *New York Times* economist, wrote, "There's no mystery about what's going on: education is mainly the responsibility of state and local governments, which are in dire fiscal straits. Adequate federal aid could have made a big difference. But while some aid has been provided, it has made up only a fraction of the shortfall. In part, that's because back in February centrist senators insisted on stripping much of that aid from the American Recovery and Reinvestment Act, a.k.a. the stimulus bill."

When Bush finally gave a measly $600 tax break to middle-class Americans, they gave it back at the gas pumps anyway, and it all went into the pockets of his oil company buddies. With one hand they put it in your pocket, with another they take it back out, crowing all the while that you got a tax cut! Charlatans!

Keep your eye on the ball, people! Look at the big picture. What matters is what you have left in your pocket at the end of the day when all your bills are paid. In most countries, people are not worrying about health care bills or the cost of college. It's covered. My point is not that tax reform isn't important. My point is that what you pay in taxes is only part of a system that is rigged against you and in favor of the super rich.

This fight has been going on for some time. "The absence of effective state, and, especially, national, restraint upon unfair money-getting has tended to create a small class of enormously wealthy and economically powerful men, whose chief object is to hold and increase their power," said Teddy Roosevelt one hundred years ago. He helped rein in that imbalance by busting monopolies and championing a progressive tax.

However, the tax code has been burdened by so many deductions and legalized favors, it doesn't operate as fairly as it should. I wonder if anyone really understands it all. Few people would argue that the federal tax code is in need of an overhaul. When Warren Buffett, one of the richest men in the world, is paying 17.7 percent and his secretary is paying 30 percent, you know something is terribly wrong.

Here's something that really galls me. After witnessing the extraordinary muscle corporations are able to flex in Washington, in essence trumping the wishes of the voters, it astounds me to discover (*Forbes* 2004) that corporations account for less than 10 percent of federal taxes paid.

According to a CNNMoney report, "Nearly two-thirds of U.S. companies and 68% of foreign corporations *do not pay federal income taxes* [emphasis mine]. . . . The Government Accountability Office (GAO) examined samples of corporate tax returns filed between 1998 and 2005. In that time period, an annual average of 1.3 million U.S. companies and 39,000 foreign companies doing business in the United States paid no income taxes—despite having a combined $2.5 trillion in revenue." The Republicans, meanwhile, want to reduce the corporate tax rate from 35 to 25 percent. If corporations actually paid that much, I might support it!

The Tax Reform Act of 1986 slashed the statutory corporate tax rate from 46 percent to 34 percent, and in the process closed enough loopholes that, according to the Multinational Monitor, the effective rate for large corporations was 26.5 percent. But, by 2003, enough new loopholes had been uncovered to bring the effective tax rate paid by major corporations down to 17.2 percent.

A middle-class family bringing home $118,000 will pay 25 percent in income tax plus another 8 percent in payroll taxes. Yet the rich can sell millions of dollars in stocks and pay a capital gains tax of only 15 percent! Baby, the rich really do get richer.

With a tax code thousands of pages long and full of loopholes, there are many people who favor a national sales tax. But the poor consume more as a percentage of their income than anyone. Is that fair? A family with an income of $50,000 would pay as much as one with an income of $500,000. It would bury the poor and middle class and be a windfall for the wealthy families.

Then there are flat taxes based on income. But a flat income tax does not address *existing* wealth. It would take at least 20 percent for a flat tax to work—probably higher. For the bottom fourth of American wage earners paying 15 percent, that would be a real kick in the teeth.

That leaves us with the progressive system, which Robert Shapiro, director of economic studies at the Progressive Foundation and vice president of the Progressive Policy Institute, explains: "A progressive tax system, however, can protect poor and middle class families from bearing the higher tax burdens entailed in a purely flat or proportional system, and in this sense, ameliorate some of the distributional inequalities achieved through our markets but based on factors other than how hard different people work. And the additional burden of progressive taxation is a reasonable price to pay by those who in some respect start with more, for the privilege of prospering relatively more under America's laws and in her markets. Bill Gates and his investors have a responsibility to not merely bear an equal share of the burden, but a greater share because they enjoy a larger share of the benefits provided by these laws and markets."

But if the wealthy are still paying less under the enlightened progressive tax, uh, Houston, we have a problem. The problem is loopholes. Man, we all love our deductions, but we sure resent the ones the other guy gets. As much as I like a simple solution, a progressive tax with minimal deductions is the best hope of the middle class.

There is much to admire about a plan from the Progressive Policy Institute that mirrors one devised by White House chief of staff Rahm Emanuel when he was a congressman and Senator Ron Wyden (D-OR). The PPI website says, "It is designed to shore up the very pillars of middle-class aspiration: paying for college, buying a first home, raising children, and saving for retirement." It eliminates sixty-eight special-interest loopholes and adds some family-friendly deductions like a $3,000-a-year incentive to students for four years of college and two years of graduate school. A second part of the plan is "a home mortgage deduction that would be available to all homeowners, not just those who itemize." Also included: "A new family tax credit would replace three existing tax incentives—the Earned Income Tax Credit, the Child Credit, and the Dependent Care Credit—and provide more benefits to more families than all of them combined. A universal pension (UP) would replace 16 existing IRA-type accounts with a single portable retirement account for all workers. It would provide a $500 stake and tax-deferred saving to workers, who could roll their 401(k) plans into their UPs when they change jobs."

And get this—the plan is budget neutral.

It's a start. But to begin to break down the imbalance of wealth, which is the only way democracy can really function, you have to beat back those who want to eliminate the death tax, something that affects just .06 percent of people. The point of taxing inherited wealth is to preserve a system that rewards hard work and innovation instead of inherited privilege. If you don't, you end up with financial royalty, and Americans decided long ago that they were done with that sort of thing. Warren Buffett said, "Dynastic wealth, the enemy of a meritocracy, is on the rise. Equality of opportunity has been on the decline. A progressive and meaningful estate tax is needed to curb the movement of a democracy toward a plutocracy."

I FAVOR LOWER TAXES THAN THE REAGAN ERA

Up until 2010, the top estate tax rate was 45 percent, with a $3.5 million deduction. However, that law expired in 2010, leaving a one-year gap until 2011, when the old rate of 55 percent will resume, unless the U.S. House and Senate can agree on another rate.

In the meantime, because the Senate was so wrapped up in the health care debate and unable to deal with the estate tax, Republicans got a reprieve—for a year, anyway. So if you are rich and lucky enough to die in 2010, your heirs will not have to pay an estate tax. Can't beat a deal like that! However, when Congress does close that gap, I say that they should move the rate to 50 percent with periodic adjustments for inflation.

But what about income tax? We need to incrementally, over the course of ten years, move the tax rate to 49 percent (from 35 percent) for those making more than $3 million. (I would also increase the tax rates on income above $1 million.) Why tax the wealthy more? Like Willie Sutton once said when asked why he robbed banks, "Because that's where the money is."

According to the Census Bureau, in 2007 the median household income was about $50,000, taxed at 25 percent. When you look at the tax rate, percentage-wise, lower-income families pay a much higher percentage than do millionaires. So asking someone making *sixty times* the median income to pay twice as much of a percentage in income taxes isn't punitive. It's still 1 percent lower than it was under Ronald Reagan!

And let's bust the myth about Reagan the tax cutter. After the gaping deficits caused by his original tax cuts, Reagan responded with what *Time* columnist Joe Klein calls "the largest peacetime tax increase in American history: the Tax Equality and Fiscal Responsibility Act, which raised $37.5 billion or 1% of GDP." Klein notes Reagan also signed a $3.3 billion tax increase and signed "another whopping tax hike designed to save Social Security."

Still, the mantra from the right is "You can't tax yourself to prosperity." Well, we've tried tax cutting our way to prosperity and ended up with the worst economic crisis since the Great Depression! I guess them good old rich boys just didn't trickle down enough. That's why we need more motivated tricklers. It's still Reaganomics, it's just *mandatory trickling* that I'm suggesting.

We could infuse Social Security with plenty of cash if we did not cap deductions on income over $106,000. In other words, anyone earning up to that amount pays the full deduction. When it comes to Social Security, the working poor pay more as a percentage in taxes than do the wealthy. While a worker making minimum wage pays 6.2 percent into the Social Security trust fund (matched by his employer), an executive making $1 million contributes only about 1 percent.

I know I sound like I don't like rich people, but I'm not about class warfare. That's not it at all. But by all measure, the rich have been doing all the *getting* in recent decades and not enough giving. I have no illusions about it; there will always be rich people and we will always have the poor, but when the imbalance between them becomes so severe, society starts to break down.

TAX THE INTERNET

Now on to the elephant in the room that we are all ignoring: the Internet. Annual sales on the Internet are well over $100 billion, most of it untaxed, and that is starting to impact your local businesses, who must add 5 to 10 percent in local and state taxes to the cost of their products. Plus, the federal government, states, and municipalities are denied revenues that they used to get. As Internet shopping grows, it will affect us in ways even Walmart couldn't—especially if we allow it to continue as a black market of sorts—a tax-free zone. Quite obviously, you cannot fund a government without tax dollars.

According to U.S. Census data, Internet sales accounted for 3.4 percent of retail sales in 2007, up a half percentage point from 2006. I know we all like the idea of paying no taxes online, but it puts local merchants at a disadvantage. It kills mom-and-pop stores just like Walmart does when it moves into a region. It's not politically popular, but we need to fairly tax Internet sales now, before more damage is done to brick-and-mortar retailers who *have* to charge state and local taxes. It's about fairness. The longer we wait, the more stores we will lose. The smart—if politically unpopular—thing to do is to implement an Internet tax plan now before this thing gets any bigger.

For once could we act before something becomes a crisis?

CAN WE AGREE ON ONE THING?

In this book there are some recurring themes—balance, for one. I also say that we should look for the things we can agree on as a nation. Balancing the budget is something I think all of us can get behind—with the exception of Dick Cheney, who said that deficits don't matter. Maybe he was speaking literally, but I believe he was speaking in the political sense. But debt is like a growing tumor. You may not feel it for a while, but eventually it kills you.

I don't think we have to do it all overnight, but to rein in the debt, I do believe we need to raise the tax rates on those who benefit the most from our system. We needn't be shy about claiming a percentage of those overseas profits that American corporations sock away while claiming a loss to the IRS. This international shell game has to stop.

It's important, too, that new expenditures and tax cuts be revenue neutral, meaning we have to find cuts or new income to balance them. This is nothing more than asking the government to live within its means just like average American citizens do.

CHAPTER ELEVEN

KICK THE MESSENGER

Become a Wiser News Consumer and a Better Citizen

WHAT IF YOU TOLD THE PARANOID WING NUTS IN THIS COUNTRY that a *foreigner* had seized control of an entire network and a publishing empire? They'd have a fit, wouldn't they? Well, spaz away, teabaggers. Australian Rupert Murdoch's News Corporation owns Fox, Harper-Collins, the *New York Post,* the *Weekly Standard, TV Guide,* DirecTV, and thirty-five TV stations. He most recently purchased the *Wall Street Journal.*

Where are the protests? I say this tongue-in-cheek, but when you think about it, isn't this an issue worth addressing? Shouldn't there be some limitation on foreign-based media ownership? But the larger concern is the monopolization of the media. I'm not saying it's a conspiracy, but the net effect is the same. You end up with fewer independent voices and more control over existing voices.

Personally, I think the loosening of FCC regulations to allow media consolidation is bad public policy. I don't think any media group should have so much potential control of the message. It's a tall order to break up these media empires, but we should. In the meantime, it's important that news consumers gain some perspective. I'm a broadcaster; I think the open microphone is democracy in action. My radio show gives the opportunity for uncensored voices to speak to millions. MSNBC has given me a great deal of latitude to do what I believe is best on *The Ed Show*—and that has given me another platform to stick up for the middle class.

But I also read newspapers and magazines, Internet sites, and every kind of credible information source I can find, and so should you. In fact, I am convinced that the more diverse your information sources are, the better the chances that you will reach many of the same conclusions I have about the world we live in. But you can't have diversity if media corporations keep gobbling up the promising small sources.

IN SEARCH OF OBJECTIVITY

Do I think there are company memos circulated to every magazine editor at Time Warner to take certain political positions? No. But if editors are aware of ownership's politics, it stands to reason they may be influenced to lean in that direction. Of course this can happen at a single mom-and-pop newspaper or radio station, and it does, but when it happens on a large scale, it becomes dangerous. It has the potential for a few powerful people to dramatically pervert the political process.

There is evidence, however, that Fox News talking points come down from on high. A memo obtained by the Huffington Post in 2006, after Democrats secured control of both houses, includes bullet points indicating that the whole strategy of the network was to mute and discredit the Democratic election victory:

- "The elections and Rumsfeld's resignations were a major event, but not the end of the world. The war on terror goes on without interruption."
- "Let's be on the lookout for any statements from the Iraqi insurgents who must be thrilled at the prospect of a Dem-controlled Congress."

- "The question of the day, and indeed for the rest of Bush's term, is what's the Dem plan for Iraq?"
- "We'll continue to work the Hamas threat to the U.S. that came hours after the election results. Just because Dems won, the war on terror isn't over."

If you watch any Fox News at all, you can see that the strategy to attack Democrats at every turn has not changed. These people couldn't spell objectivity even if you waterboarded them and spotted them every letter but the Y.

We report. You decide. . . .

Fine, I've decided Fox News is completely full of shit.

Let's move on to one of the most obvious reasons for breaking up media monopolies. Clear Channel, which features Rush Limbaugh, dominates radio with more than nine hundred stations. If FCC deregulation had led to nine hundred stations broadcasting me, can you imagine the howls of protest? How in the world can we expect democracy to survive when the message is so consolidated and so many people can be duped at one time?

Make no mistake. The right wing sound machine is alive and well and still dominant. The main reason the Democrats are in power is because the Bush-Cheney Corporation was so obviously inept and Barack Obama's candidacy so brilliantly orchestrated. I'll say this now: Unless the Democrats unite behind the president, grow some balls, and stand up to the right wing sound machine and their big money ownership, the conservatives will be back in power faster than Dick Cheney can steal candy from a baby.

Phil Donahue told *Democracy Now!*, "We have more [TV] outlets now, but most of them sell the Bowflex machine. The rest of them are Jesus and jewelry. There really isn't diversity in the media anymore. Dissent? Forget about it."

John Whitehead, a constitutional attorney and president of the Rutherford Institute, warns, "Truth is often lost when we fail to distinguish between opinion and fact, and that is the danger we now face as a society. Anyone who relies exclusively on television/cable news hosts and political commentators for actual knowledge of the world is making a serious mistake. Unfortunately, since Americans have by and large become non-readers, television has become their prime source of so-called news."

Fox News (We report. You fall for it.) has figured out that there is big money in cheerleading for conservatives. They understand that people like to hear a message that reinforces and validates their personal beliefs, no matter how misanthropic they may be. MSNBC went in the other direction with programming that largely speaks to moderates and liberals. Is any of this journalism? Not in any classic sense—especially at Fox News, where I truly find them to be propagandists for conservatism while intoning that they are "fair and balanced." Yeah, and the pope is a Baptist. The thing is, they're just so *dishonest*. Yes, dishonest, because the only other possibility is that they are deluded, and I just cannot believe that a whole network can be *that* crazy.

Michael Massing of the *Columbia Journalism Review* said, "It seems clear to me that Fox is engaged in a calculated and determined campaign to destroy the Obama presidency—a campaign that also happens to be good for its ratings. It's true that, where Fox has a strong rightward tilt, MSNBC has a strong leftward one." He concludes, "But the network [MSNBC] just doesn't seem to feature the conspiratorial looniness or corrosive fear-mongering that pervades Fox."

THE NEED FOR DIVERSITY AND EDUCATION

Clearly, one of the most important things we can do is to start breaking up the media monopolies. Once we have diversity of ownership, there will be diversity of programming, and I can damn sure tell you that will make for a better democracy. Monopolies can stagnate an economy every bit as much as socialism. Media monopolies are nothing short of dangerous.

There was a time in the seventies—with Vietnam and Watergate and the Pentagon Papers—when good journalism was prevalent, we were all operating with the same facts, and I trusted my fellow Americans to come to logical conclusions. Sure, conservative and liberal philosophies may lead to different approaches to government, but in the end, I felt as if we all had the same motive, which was to help make America a better place. I just don't see that much anymore.

Many journalists approach their jobs with the same sense of integrity a member of the clergy might. However, there seem to be fewer journalists and more commentators in the profession with journalism backgrounds. Something that ought to be seriously considered is funding high school journalism programs at schools that cannot afford them, not necessarily with the mission of producing journalists, but the mission of producing better-educated news consumers who have an understanding of the traditional ethics of the profession. We teach government, but neglect the crucial Fourth Estate of Democracy—a free press.

I'm one of those new voices in a new media frontier that is at its best advocacy journalism and at its worst propaganda. At MSNBC, I see us as advocacy journalists. At Fox News, I believe them to be willfully misleading and dishonest often enough to be called propagandists.

I think it was healthy for the Obama administration to go on the offensive against Fox News and challenge their misinformation, because it drew attention to the severe slant and inherent dishonesty of the network. The hardcore right wing Fox viewers won't be swayed by the White House offensive, but more independent minds might be jolted enough to at least reexamine the way Fox does business. Lawrence O'Donnell observed on MSNBC that it is typical for the relationship between media and politicians to be adversarial. Fox News, he said, has an adversarial relationship with *the facts*.

In the last thirty years, conservatives have been eager to embrace propaganda techniques to discredit their enemies. The recipe is: Keep the message simple and repeat it often. It is no secret that in the eighties, conservatives began a whisper campaign about the "liberal media." They repeated this so often, people came to accept it as fact. (As if conservatives were being banned from journalism schools.) The whole idea was to discredit what was largely a very credible messenger. The problem with conservatives is they view *the facts* as liberal!

FOR BETTER OR WORSE, THE AGE OF ADVOCACY JOURNALISM

I say if we're going to do advocacy journalism, let's admit it. But Fox News has morphed to all-out attack journalism against the Democrats while claiming to be fair and balanced. The only real exception to the rule is Bill O'Reilly, who does defend the Democrats sometimes when the attacks become too ridiculous.

I have taken prominent Democrats to task objectively, from Bill Clinton to Barack Obama, but I have also unabashedly advocated strongly for national health care. I won't call what I do journalism in the strictest sense of the word, but even so, that does not absolve me of responsibility as a broadcaster to be intellectually honest.

Is it possible to advocate and also be credible? I think so. I have used a major cable network and a national radio show to advocate public policy. But here's what separates me (and I believe most everyone at MSNBC) from the people at Fox News: I speak out the way I do because *I believe in it,* not because it is the party line. I have always spoken with my heart, and what I believe to be the truth, and it has cost me dearly sometimes.

TOUGH LOVE FOR THE ONES YOU LOVE

You think it's fun to have Bill Clinton mad at you—or even longtime friends? It's not. When I felt he was resorting to underhanded political innuendo, I told Chris Matthews on MSNBC's *Hardball,* "Bill Clinton is lying about Barack Obama's record when it comes to the war, and when it comes to this comment about Republicans and Reagan. [I felt Clinton misrepresented a comment Obama had made about Reagan.] And you know what Democrats are being reminded of when Clinton gets out on the stump? He lied ten years ago about Monica Lewinsky, and he's lying about a very viable candidate and somebody who could really bring change in this country. He is embarrassing for Democrats."

The thing is I love and admire Bill Clinton, and I appreciate the loyalty he showed to Hillary (who would make a tremendous president in her own right), but he went too far, and I felt I had to challenge him. I was the guy with a microphone who said what many others were thinking, and since I have been a longtime supporter of Bill Clinton, my criticism had credibility. Of course, in politics, you can say, "he isn't telling the truth," or "his statement does not reflect the facts," or other niceties, but if you say someone lied, those are fighting words.

I've said many more positive things about Bill Clinton than negative, but I understand how hurtful my comment was to him. I hope he will get past it. He's a complex, brilliant, and yes, flawed man. As a guy who has plenty of flaws myself, I wasn't being holier than thou. I was serving my conscience, and hopefully the democratic process. Being committed to telling the truth means you have to be willing to burn some bridges. I'm no different than anyone else; I want to be liked. But I want to be able to look myself in the eye every morning. It's about credibility. If that means I don't get a Christmas card from Bill Clinton this year, so be it.

By following my conscience instead of a party platform, I am liberated to say what's on my mind. Everybody knows that's the deal with me. I'm not always right, but my heart's right. Integrity is how I got here, and it's coming with me when they bounce my ass out on the street—and hey, let's face it, it happens to everyone in this business.

While conservative ownership and conservative programming continues to dominate, one can still find great journalists and great journalism at the big three networks and some cable and Internet venues. The fact that my national radio show was able to grow to one hundred stations in this environment should give you hope.

And there is some real fresh air in media today. On the Internet, the Daily Kos, Huffington Post, FactCheck.org, Media Matters, and MoveOn .org are among several sites that provide a reality check to the right wing sound machine. On television, Comedy Central's Jon Stewart and Stephen Colbert deliver truth, wickedly and ironically dissecting the day's news. Sometimes a raised eyebrow from Jon Stewart says it all.

WAITING FOR THE JOURNALISM ENLIGHTENMENT

Just as campaign donations create conflict of interest and credibility issues, so does the media formula in which journalism is funded by advertising. While anyone who has worked in radio and television knows there has traditionally been a clear line between the editorial and the advertising departments, it's only natural that news consumers might have suspicions about the integrity and autonomy of the news department. Indeed, news outlets have been compromised by bean counters in many ways. Few networks spend the money on foreign bureaus anymore because journalism has taken a backseat to stockholder profits. I understand better than anyone the importance of turning a profit with a show, but if you have to sell out your principles or core purpose, what have you accomplished?

As a matter of credibility, *Mother Jones* magazine, one of the last bastions of fierce journalistic integrity, survives without ad revenue. They do seek donations for their watchdog journalism. The *Nation,* edited by my friend and frequent contributor to my shows Katrina vanden Heuvel, has a similar model. Public radio and television is funded by a combination of government dollars and donations. (Of course, those government dollars make it vulnerable to the political power of the day.)

As a news consumer, would you pay for a subscription to a radio program, a television program, or a magazine if you were convinced you were getting objective journalism? If you get HBO or satellite radio, you are already paying a premium not to be interrupted by commercials. Isn't that what TiVo is all about—the convenience of getting media without the intrusion of advertising?

Perhaps the next step is for news consumers who lament the state of journalism to put their money where their democracy is and support subscriber-based journalism. This is the next frontier, and I believe you will see someone with deep pockets and a dedication to real journalism give this a try. Imagine if Ted Turner had created twenty-four-hour cable news based completely on subscriber revenues? What he did by launching CNN was revolutionary. Had he had the vision to make it subscriber-based only, it could have been transformational. I don't intend to be unfair to Ted Turner by asking a visionary to be even more of a genius! I admire him a great deal, and what might work now may not have worked then.

No matter what, the minute one of these subscriber-based, no-commercial publications or broadcasts becomes profitable, it will get imitators/competitors. Ideally, the competition will be to see who can be most objective. But, human nature being what it is, sensationalism might well creep in. While journalists are considered the watchdogs of society, who watches the media? *You do.*

Turner, who once called Rupert Murdoch the most dangerous man in the world, doesn't like what he sees. "The media is too concentrated, too few people own too much," he says. "There's really five companies that control 90 percent of what we read, see and hear. It's not healthy."

Some have cursed Turner's invention of the 24/7 news cycle, but you cannot blame him for the inability of news consumers to keep up. The incredible number of news sources may seem overwhelming, but being an informed citizen is your responsibility. You have to determine how credible a news source is.

A vote is an awesome responsibility. You ought to study for an election like it's a test. Actually, it is. It is a test of democracy, and judging from the election of some goofballs like Representative Michele Bachmann (D-MN), who is a regular on *The Ed Show* segment entitled "Psycho Talk" for her bizarre rants, we need to hit the books a little harder. God help us if she and Glenn Beck ever have a love child. He will goosestep out of the womb and cry a lot.

While we wait as if for Godot, for a new enlightenment in journalism, we should concentrate on breaking up the media monopolies. If we don't open the airwaves to more owners and more diversity, the conservatives will exercise more control over the microphone, the press, the Internet, and the message itself.

As a progressive, you have to be smart enough and curious enough to get to the facts, and you can't be shy about sharing them and correcting misconceptions and lies. You have to challenge the Righties at every turn, at every coffee shop, on every talk show, on every editorial page— just like they do us. Complacency will kill the progressive movement, so pay attention and stay active.

CHAPTER TWELVE

TERM LIMITS AND A THIRD PARTY

Stop Big Money from Trumping Your Vote

CHANGE. NEARLY 67 MILLION— 53 PERCENT OF VOTING AMERICANS— voted for Barack Obama in 2008, but instead of change we have experienced gridlock and a rude awakening, discovering that our votes don't count as much as the big money interests that really call the shots in Washington.

I've said this before: I fear big business far more than big government. The reason is pretty simple. Government is restricted by more rules. Unless you regulate monsters like the insurance industry, energy companies—you name the industry—you get what we have now, behemoths able *and willing* to put their interests above those of the country in perpetuity. All elected officials know they can be targeted in the next election and defeated by these ruthless people.

Unless we get serious about breaking up the stranglehold big business monopolies have on our political system, they will render this democracy unrecognizable.

Dwight Eisenhower saw it coming and warned about the "military industrial complex." What few people know is that Eisenhower's original draft warned against the "military industrial *congressional* complex."

But, having enjoyed a good working relationship with Congress, he decided to exit on a positive note. The unholy entanglement of big business and big government continues.

There are plenty of Democrats who have been compromised by big money, but as the party of deregulation and K-Street bribery, the Republicans have been the greatest enablers.

Throughout this book, I have illustrated the ways the system has been rigged to transfer the wealth from the middle class to the wealthy and corporate elite. Since Ronald Reagan took office, according to census statistics from 1979 to 2005, the top 5 percent of Americans have increased their wealth *81 percent* while the bottom 20 percent, the American workers, saw their income decline 1 percent.

Sadly, right wing propaganda has convinced many in the middle class that the enemy is the poor, that entitlements for the poor are the problem. Yet somehow entitlements for corporate America are never mentioned.

BIG MONEY INFLUENCE PEDDLERS

Why is change so slow in coming? The truth is that even though we changed dealers, the deck has been increasingly stacked against the middle class by influence peddlers for years. Changing this will take more time and more effort. The sad fact is that many politicians worry more about being reelected than they do about doing the right thing in Washington. They know if they take on these big money interests, they will not only lose their campaign donations, but their opponent will get them. Campaign advertising works, and most of the time, the guy with the biggest war chest wins. According to Common Cause, an organization seeking election reform, "The average winning U.S. Senate race in 2006 cost nearly $10 million and the average winning House race that year cost $1.3 million. The decisions about who runs and who wins in our democracy increasingly come down to big money and special interests, not regular voters."

The obvious answer is to prohibit corporate donations. However, an 1886 Supreme Court decision, *Santa Clara County v. Southern Pacific Railroad,* dubiously granted corporations the same rights as individuals. Direct contributions from corporations were limited after it was learned that Teddy Roosevelt's 1904 presidential campaign was funded in part by direct contributions from the insurance industry.

But today, corporations and unions form political action committees to circumvent the law forbidding direct contributions. So these PACs write the campaign checks, and the system goes merrily on. Industries continue to flood Washington with lobbyists and money. Jeffrey Kaplan, of ReclaimDemocracy.org, writes, "Democracy is at risk when we permit vast amounts of money . . . to buy power over the political process itself. . . . In other words, the money big donors withhold, not just money they give, helps keep legislators in line. The result is a 'chilling effect' . . . whereby certain policies are not even discussed for fear of alienating wealthy donors."

The McCain-Feingold finance reform bill was passed and put into place in 2003 to limit soft money and issue advocacy ads, but it was like building a dam that doesn't reach the other side. Special interests found another loophole with the increased use of tax-exempt 527 groups, like the Swift Boaters who slimed John Kerry. These 527s are not subject to the same contribution limits as PACs, and the courts say they are legal as long as they do not coordinate their efforts with a candidate or party.

This is a huge loophole, leaving room for all kinds of mischief. The 527s can sling mud while the candidate they support can throw up his hands and say disingenuously, "What can I do to stop them?" That is exactly what George W. Bush did while John Kerry's Vietnam service was discredited in 2004.

And now, ominously, the Supreme Court has decided by a 5–4 vote, in *Citizens United v. Federal Election Commission,* that it is unconstitutional to prohibit direct contributions by corporations and unions. The floodgates of corporate money will be opened wider as a hundred years of election reforms are rolled back.

Are campaign contributions, as some would argue, an extension of free speech? If so, it is obvious that big money has quite a megaphone.

GOVERNMENT FOR THE RICH BY THE RICH

Ideally, campaigns would be wholly publicly funded to keep corporations, unions, and wealthy individuals from contributing. Nor should we allow wealthy individuals to fund, beyond a modest amount, their own campaigns, in essence to buy elections. What Mayor Bloomberg did in New York, first by extending term limits to suit his personal quest for another term and then by funding his 2008 campaign to the tune of $102 million, is a slap in the face of democracy. I don't question his intent, but his method sets a terrible precedent.

Any man or woman's opportunity to serve should not be dictated by money. Otherwise, you get a government by the rich for the rich—people who are completely out of touch with the middle class. According to Politico.com, there are 237 millionaires in Congress! Forty-four percent of those in Congress are millionaires! And these are the folks looking out for you and me? Tell me again the fairy tale about this being a democracy.

It's a plutocracy.

Along with publicly funded campaigns, the public airwaves should be used to broadcast debates. You see, the airwaves are owned by the public and only licensed to broadcasters with the provision that they serve the public good. Setting aside some time for debates is certainly in the public interest.

Because we are asking the fox to guard the henhouse, getting big money out of politics any time soon isn't realistic. But a good first step would be to forbid or strictly limit out-of-state campaign contributions.

Should out-of-state interests be able to buy U.S. senators and congress-people simply by contributing more than can be raised in the actual legislative district to be represented?

I'm not saying every senator and congressperson is bought and paid for, but all of them are influenced at one level or another, and all it takes is for a few of them in key positions to gum up the works. Even though for a short time the Democrats had a sixty-seat majority in the Senate, just a handful of conservative Democrats had the power to control the fate of health care and other legislation.

There are some politicians I respect—people I know to have good hearts and good intentions—but even then I am disappointed because I see them calculate their votes sometimes based on how it might affect their reelection, imagining corporately funded campaigns against them, and they lose the courage to do the right thing. Noble, principled votes *do* still happen in Washington. And even votes for compromise are not always sellouts, but just part of the give-and-take you have to have.

DISTRUST IN THE ELECTORAL PROCESS

After Barack Obama was elected president, people began saying that this was proof that, finally, all parents could honestly tell their children that *anyone* really could become president. But, hell, *Obama* didn't prove that; President Rainman did—twice!

I'll say this about the Republicans—they're not worth beans at governing, but they sure know how to win. There were enough conservative zealots in place to heist an election in Florida in 2000 and possibly another in 2004, when the exit polls indicated John Kerry would be the winner. With all the suspicions surrounding our democratic process, specifically after the debacle in Florida, when we criticize elections around the globe, especially in Afghanistan, we look both naïve and hypocritical.

Jimmy Carter said once, "The best way to enhance freedom in other lands is to demonstrate here that our democratic system is worthy of emulation." If that's the case, we have some work to do.

As a Democrat, I always had the feeling that Barack Obama would have to win big in 2008 so they couldn't steal the election. Maybe it's paranoia, but after eight years of Bush and Cheney, it is *justified* paranoia.

The neocons have shown they will do anything to win. They had no compunction about manipulating the public through fear to win. Didn't you get suspicious as the election approached that suddenly the specter of terrorism was reintroduced just to remind Americans what a dangerous world it is? It came as no surprise when former Bush Homeland Security secretary Tom Ridge revealed in 2009 that he was pressured to amp up the threat level on the eve of the 2004 election. (He later tried to back away from those comments.) Was that brazen manipulation enough to swing the election to Bush? It surely didn't hurt.

EXCUSE ME, COULD I GET A RECEIPT, PLEASE?

Maybe Dubya really did win both times, but the fact that so many doubts remain should tell us the system needs more transparency. I don't like the way my vote just disappears into thin air and presumably to a secure hard drive. Computer scientist Avi Rubin told National Public Radio, "I think that just as much that I'm worried about it being rigged, I'm also worried about an unintentional software error causing the wrong outcome to come out. And the biggest problem is that, regardless of whether anything goes wrong with the machines, we don't know that it didn't. And there are voting systems that are possible, you know, paper-based systems where if you suspect that something went wrong, there's a way to check. You can perform a recount, so you can perform an audit. The problem with these electronic systems is that if you suspect that something went wrong, and show me an election where someone didn't suspect that something went wrong, there's nothing that you can do about it."

As former Minnesota governor Jesse Ventura put it, "I can get a receipt from an ATM, but I can't get one from a voting machine?" While the Democrats are in power, they had better use the opportunity to ensure the process is honest and transparent; otherwise don't be surprised in our next election to discover that Hamid Karzai has won.

Many Americans have already concluded that their vote really doesn't count, and what we have witnessed in Washington in recent years certainly adds credibility to their view, but if the day ever comes that we lose the trust of the overwhelming majority of voters, we will lose this democracy.

A CASE FOR TERM LIMITS

Senator Barbara Boxer (D-CA) chided me one day on *The Ed Show:* "Ed, you're just being too hard on the Democrats!" I like her a lot and I think she likes me, so it came across as a motherly scolding. Maybe sometimes I am too hard on the Democrats, but I don't mind being told that. I'll take it as a badge of honor and a testament to my independent thinking.

I believe you have to hold their feet to the fire.

Sending good people off to Washington without someone peeking over their shoulder is like sending drunk college boys to the whorehouse with a pocket full of money and no curfew. Somebody's bound to get screwed. And when you consider that in recent years there has been an unprecedented transfer of wealth from the poor and middle class to the wealthy, check your pants. They're probably down around your knees. A compromised media is the date-rape drug of choice.

I used to question term limits, believing that if we turned over lawmakers too quickly, bureaucracies would become the real power. It is now evident that everyone eventually ends up in the same bed anyway. I think the country is ready for term limits and a real citizen government—people who have to return to the trenches after two terms—and not professional politicians. There is certain clarity of thought and a courage that comes from a man or woman with nothing to lose.

And if we're really serious, let's send them home *without* lifetime benefits. Not to punish but to motivate. If politicians actually had to go back after a few years and live in the messes they have made, we would have national health care, a four-day workweek, no wars, and free beer.

Rare is the individual who does not develop a sense of entitlement after being in Washington for a while. Politicians start to believe that the rules don't apply to them. The president had a hard time finding appointees that didn't have something embarrassing in their backgrounds. Tom Daschle and Tim Geithner had tax issues. They were followed by a string of appointees who stepped aside for one embarrassing reason or another. I think the president must have felt a little like Diogenes, wandering the streets of ancient Athens with a lantern, searching for an honest man.

I applaud the Obama administration's effort to try to appoint only "squeaky clean" politicians, but seemingly there is no such thing. Even the best of individuals have potential conflicts of interest. Few would be able to escape the perception of impropriety even where there is none.

MORE PARTIES, MORE DEMOCRACY

So far, I have offered two basic solutions for improving government and the electoral process: get money out of the equation and enact term limits.

Failing that, there is another avenue. I believe the system would function much better if there were more political parties. If a third party did emerge, even if it managed less than 20 percent of the seats in Congress, its mere presence in Washington would hopefully restore old-fashioned "what's best for the country"–style debate. A minority can have the power of the majority as power brokers—as evidenced by the clout wielded by the Blue Dog Democrats during the health care debate. We have conservative Democrats and moderate Republicans, and as insufferable as the Blue Dog Democrats can be, their willingness to buck their party isn't always bad. In the long run, that kind of diversity is healthy. But when it comes to getting things done quickly, it's the shits.

I know liberals were frustrated with Ralph Nader because he may have taken enough votes to cost Gore the election in 2000. It's a weak argument. The fact is, Al Gore could not carry his home state of Tennessee. Do I think the Supreme Court robbed Al Gore? Sure. Any court that refused to allow a complete recount botched it. But any football player will tell you that you never want to let your opponent get close enough that a referee's decision decides the outcome. Even McGovern won his home state.

In comparison, while it seemingly took forever for the courts to sort through the Al Franken/Norm Coleman election in Minnesota, they took enough time to get it right.

If there was ever a classic case to show that your vote matters, it was in that senate race. Franken prevailed by just a couple hundred votes. That gave the Democrats a chance at a sixty-seat majority in the Senate! A few hundred votes shifted the balance of power in Washington.

But even that kind of majority has not broken the gridlock, and I think both parties are treading on thin ice with American voters. I think both parties are going to discover that if they cannot govern, the American people will begin to support a third party. Maybe even a fourth party. If so, those parties will dilute the power of the existing parties—and it's hard to argue that it is not a good thing.

Ralph Nader's third-party run may have hurt Al Gore, but Ross Perot's third-party candidacy opened the door for Bill Clinton by taking votes from George Herbert Walker Bush. So Democrats and Republicans alike at one time or another have resented third parties. But, as Americans, we may discover that a viable third party is the element that revitalizes this democracy.

I'm not looking to upset the applecart for no reason. If the Democrats can get it done, I'll be happy. But if push comes to shove, my allegiance is to the middle class of America. The American citizen is the collateral damage in this political war. As jobs are lost, houses foreclosed upon, and credit card companies and insurance companies continue to pillage, they're fiddling like Nero in Washington, D.C.

I MUST BE CRAZY, BUT I STILL HAVE HOPE

FRIENDS, WE'VE COVERED A GREAT DEAL OF GROUND IN THIS BOOK. I haven't pulled any punches and my knuckles are sore, and many of the issues we've covered continue to unravel, but I hope I have provided some optimism, too. If you are a regular listener to *The Ed Schultz Show* on the radio or a viewer of *The Ed Show* on MSNBC, you know that I tell it like it is. I tell the unvarnished truth so much my chairs have wood rot!

And I'm a little frustrated because so much opportunity lies before us and the change we fought for has come so slowly. But that's America. Participating in this great democracy has never been easy. Anyone who thinks otherwise has fallen for illusions from the shiny pages of the lesser history books, the ones disinfected of all the blood, sweat, tears, and pain. All good things in life require a heavy lift, so roll up your sleeves. We are not done yet.

I have to keep reminding myself, and you should, too, that in many ways, we are pioneers. Let me explain. I started this book talking about the importance of flying ahead of the airplane—about knowing where you are going, about having a vision for the future. The fact that you are reading this book tells me you share my vision of a greater America, a country that rises higher to achieve justice and one that bends lower in compassion for those left behind.

Here's the thing about being a pioneer, a visionary. . . . It's a frustrating business. You eventually discover that it takes the rest of the good people a while to catch up. The good news is: They eventually do. But by that time, you will be flying ahead to the next thing. God bless the visionaries!

Man, I was so frustrated that we kept losing elections to George W. Bush by a hair. Gore . . . Kerry . . . *We worked so hard!* I had this vision of what these good men could help us accomplish. And maybe I was like a lot of folks, thinking that the transformational statement America made in electing an African-American Democrat meant that things were going to get easier. After all, hadn't America evolved?

Instead—*skreeech!*—what the hell? Is that another roadblock up ahead? It turns out, along with an increasingly strident Republican opposition, there were conservative Democrats blocking the way. Now, that doesn't make them bad people—despite my intemperate remarks from time to time—maybe they're just reflecting the districts from which they come. When you have a big tent, along with the donkeys, you get a few goats and a skunk or two. That is both the strength and weakness of the Democratic Party. (The Republicans, on the other hand, have this itty-bitty tent filled with elephants and fat cats. No wonder they're so grumpy.)

Nor has President Obama lived up to his potential. Inspirational? Blessedly so. Smart? As a whip. But can he kick asses when the time comes? That remains to be seen. And on some issues, in my opinion, the time has come and gone. Take off the wingtips, Mr. President, and grab those steel-toed boots. You won nine Bush states! That's a mandate.

As hard as I have been on the president, I know that all of us—even one as gifted as Barack Obama—have strengths and weakness. In the end, we are only human. Some of us are closet smokers. Others take a wide stance in airport bathrooms. Greatness is never independent of flaws, and often greatness is achieved *in spite of them*. Let us not build our pedestals too high, because the fall can do you in. I continue to admire and support the president and have faith that Barack Obama can become a great leader. Heck, I'm an American! That was my hope for George W. Bush. I wanted America to succeed! Nothing has changed for me in that respect.

The opposition tactic is to throw a wrench into the gears of government, then blame the driver when things stall. That's not an upright thing to do, but that's what passes for statesmanship these days, and that's why Barack Obama is at the wheel of a stalled car of state from time to time. It's easy for the attention-deficit media to fall into the trap of thinking that maybe the progressive movement has failed. Not at all! It all comes down to power. There are just not enough progressives in positions of power. Not every Democrat is a progressive, just as every Republican is not a close-minded right wing zealot. So—I know it's difficult to have patience, believe me!—but don't get down over the slow pace of things. Now is the time for another big push. Many things come down to which side wants it more.

As I said earlier in this book, we need educated news consumers because those are the people who become engaged voters. The blessing in all of this mess is that many American voters have emerged with a much deeper understanding about the way Washington works or, in some cases, how it doesn't. We have watched health care bills born, all shiny and clean in committees, then seen the various incarnations pulled apart, amended, and kneaded all back together again. What was for many of us a mysterious process has been revealed for what it is—a painstaking, political, bare-knuckle brawl between ideologies, a brawl that's taking place—and taking so long—at a time when the middle class of America needs prompt support and attention or else it may entirely fade away. Otto von Bismarck famously said, "Laws are like sausages. It's better not to see them being made." But I disagree. I think the more we understand about the way the system works, the better our chances are to reform it.

The Barack Obama administration has been a whirlwind tour of the legislative process, blind alleys and all. Most presidencies have a rough first year. Barack Obama has had one of the most trying, but in spite of it all, his leadership kept the economy from crashing. Even if Republicans won't give him credit for any of that now, historians will later. And even though we fell short of getting national health care in his first year in office, Obama made great headway with health care reform. He has begun restoring America's standing in the world. He has reached out to other countries, and they've reached back. And he's managed not to invade anyone! Holy smokes! That should count for something. But this is America. We want more, and we want it now!

Here's the reality check: All of the struggle we've witnessed during Obama's first year is part of the democratic process. On rare occasions in America's history, transformational legislation has happened seemingly overnight, but most of our progress has been measured in three yards and a cloud of dust. Civil rights didn't come overnight, nor has racism disappeared. Some profound changes come with the stroke of a pen, like Medicare and Social Security. Wars start and end with a pen. Other change is measured by generations.

Endure, my friend. Keep working. Keep the faith.

The radicalism and festering hate that has infected the right casts a shadow over the light America represents. Likewise, the extremists on the left have often tainted the process with uncivil ugliness. That kind of behavior stems from fear and frustration, and I understand that, but we have to rise above it.

The stranglehold the two parties have on power seems to have choked the life out of progress, but time will tell. Maybe enough leadership will emerge to break that gridlock. I have hopes.

If old-fashioned fiscal conservatism ever returns to the Republican Party—and don't mistake a mindless, ugly attack on social programs and the poor for any sort of fiscal restraint!—I would welcome back the Republicans. If the part of the Republican Party that was slow to rattle sabers and that championed personal freedom emerges again, America would be better for it. We can balance the pragmatism of what once was the party of Lincoln with the progressive vision that strives to better the human condition. We can embrace good ideas, no matter from where they sprout.

I will continue to support the Democratic Party for now, but as I have shown by my unsparing criticism of some Democrats, I'm not in the tank for anyone that isn't on the right side of the issues. I'm on the airwaves every day to make a difference for the American family, for the middle-class worker. My roots are in the middle class. The middle class are my people.

I was honored when asked to run in North Dakota Senator Byron Dorgan's place, after his announced retirement at the end of his term, but I realized I can best serve the middle class from where I am now.

So where do we go from here?

The president once said something compelling and thought-provoking that I think we ought to take to heart: "This is our time. . . . We are the ones we are waiting for."

What he is saying is, it's time for us to lead—time for *you* to lead. There are many ways to do that. Get involved. Speak up at the coffee shop. Write letters to the editor. Write letters to your legislators (typed and original, my colleague Chris Matthews says). Support American businesses when you can.

Our mission is to keep working to elect progressive leaders wherever we find them. Vote for the right person who will do the right things— someone who will do the bidding of the voters, and not of the corporations. And if you cannot find the right person, *be* that person.

Understand that there will be some setbacks. So what? That's life. Huddle up and here we go . . . three more yards and a cloud of dust. As long as we keep coming to the line, the game isn't over. Progress may not come as fast as we, in our impatience and impertinence, demand. But if we are patient and persistent, it will come.

Joseph Marshall III, a Lakota author who grew up in the Dakotas, wrote, "Each step, no matter how difficult, is one step closer to the top of the hill. . . . The weakest step toward the top of the hill, toward the sunrise, toward hope, is stronger than the fiercest storm. . . . Keep going."

That's the mission.

Keep going.

Index